A Workbook of Acceptance-Based Approaches for Weight Concerns

This three-part workbook offers a concise and forgiving research-based guide to clients' difficulties with sustained weight loss. Part 1 is a review of your client's previous efforts at weight control and image change, as well as information and a review of research to help your client understand why weight loss might not have worked in the past. Part 2 contains information and exercises to help your client develop a new acceptance of their body and their relationship with food, as well as tools to develop mindfulness and self-compassion. Part 3 will help your client identify, experiment with, and commit to values related to food, appearance, and other important areas of life, tackling troublesome mental and practical barriers along the way.

Margit I. Berman is an assistant professor of psychiatry at the Geisel School of Medicine at Dartmouth and associate professor of clinical psychology at the Minnesota School of Professional Psychology at Argosy University. She was the recipient of the 2015 Hitchcock Foundation Scholars Career Development award for her research and development of the *Accept Yourself!* intervention for women with obesity and depression. She is the past chair of the Society for Counseling Psychology's Section for the Promotion of Psychotherapy Science, and is on the editorial boards of *The Counseling Psychologist* and the *Journal of Counseling Psychology*.

A Workbook of Acceptance-Based Approaches for Weight Concerns

The *Accept Yourself!* Framework

Margit I. Berman

First published 2018
by Routledge
711 Third Avenue, New York, NY 10017

and by Routledge
2 Park Square, Milton Park, Abingdon, Oxon, OX14 4RN

Routledge is an imprint of the Taylor & Francis Group, an informa business

© 2018 Taylor & Francis

The right of Margit I. Berman to be identified as author of this work has been asserted by her in accordance with sections 77 and 78 of the Copyright, Designs and Patents Act 1988.

All rights reserved. No part of this book may be reprinted or reproduced or utilised in any form or by any electronic, mechanical, or other means, now known or hereafter invented, including photocopying and recording, or in any information storage or retrieval system, without permission in writing from the publishers.

Trademark notice: Product or corporate names may be trademarks or registered trademarks, and are used only for identification and explanation without intent to infringe.

Library of Congress Cataloging-in-Publication Data
A catalog record for this title has been requested

ISBN: 978-1-138-06875-9 (hbk)
ISBN: 978-1-138-06878-0 (pbk)
ISBN: 978-1-315-15764-1 (ebk)

Typeset in Syntax
by Out of House Publishing

To Ruth Berman, who encouraged me to write.

Contents

Acknowledgments x
Introduction: Who This Book is for and How to Use it xi
   How to Use This Book xi
   I Can Never Accept My Body at This Weight: Is This Book Right for Me? xi
   A Word about Language xii
   Reference xiv

PART 1 YOUR WEIGHT, YOUR BODY: CAN YOU CONTROL IT? (AND WHY NOT?)   1

1 Your Body Struggle: Evaluating Your Progress Thus Far   3
   What Has Your Struggle Cost You? 3
      Worksheet: What Has This Problem Cost You? 4
   Your Body Over Time 5
      Worksheet: Your Body Timeline 6
   What Have You Already Tried to Solve This Problem? 7
      Worksheet: What Strategies Have You Tried to Solve Your Problem? 9
   Reference 12

2 The Surprising Truth about Weight Loss   13
   The Science of Weight Loss: It's Not What You Think 13
   Why Might Dieting Lead to Weight Gain? 14
   How Bad Is Obesity for Your Health? 15
   Are the Health Effects of Weight Affected by Culture and Discrimination? 17
   References 17

3 The Magic Wand   19
   My Magic Wand Fantasy 19
      Worksheet: Your Dreams and Values 22
      Worksheet: Dreams and Values Map 24
   Is *Accept Yourself!* Right for Me if I Have to Diet for My Health? 25
      A Health At Every Size® Approach to Health 25
      Making Health Changes 26
      Worksheet: My Health Screening Results (at the Beginning of *Accept Yourself!*) 26
      Worksheet: My Doctor and I Brainstormed a List of Health Behaviors to Address My Health Concerns 27
      One Health Change 28
      My Health Change Goal (for Readers with a Specific Health Concern *Only*) 29
      Worksheet: Health Change Goals and Barriers 30

CONTENTS

    Bookmark This Page! 31
    Worksheet: One-Month Bookmark Check-In 31
    End-of-Book Check-In 32
    Worksheet: My Health Screening Results (at the End of *Accept Yourself!*) 32
  References 32

PART 2   BODY ACCEPTANCE   33

4 Turning Down Programming, Tuning in to Your Body   35

  There Is a Reason It Is Called Programming 36
    Worksheet: My Programming 38
    Orwell's Circus Dog 40
    Albert Ellis and *The Folklore of Sex* 40
  Turning Down Programming, Tuning in to Your Body 41
    A Different Kind of Diet 41
    Worksheet: Media Diet 41
    What Does Your Body Really Look like? 44
    Worksheet: Silhouette Tracing: What Did I Observe? 44
    Worksheet: The Mindful Mirror: My Observations 46
    Mindful Movement 46
  Is There a Bomb in Your Mind? 47
    Worksheet: Envisioning a Bomb 47
  References 48

5 From Mindfulness to Self-Acceptance   49

  Building Acceptance by Experiencing 49
    Amy's Painful Situations 50
    Worksheet: My Painful Situations 51
    My Painful Situations 52
    Worksheet: The Acceptance Mountain 53
    Avoidance in the Midst of Acceptance 53
    Worksheet: Acceptance Practice #1 54

6 Producing Your Own Programming   55

  Worksheet: Acceptance Practice #2 55
  Difficulties with Self-Acceptance: Size Discrimination 56
    Dealing with Size Discrimination at the Doctor's Office 57
  Producing Your Own Programming 57
    Resources for Programming the No-Self-Judgment Channel 58
    Books 58
    Websites 59
    Worksheet: How Will You Create a Self-Judgment-Free Channel and a Body
      Disparagement-Free Zone? 60
  References 60

PART 3   CAN YOU LIVE THE LIFE YOU'VE ALWAYS WANTED, IN THE BODY YOU HAVE NOW?   61

7 The Value of Feeding Yourself   63

  Worksheet: Acceptance Practice #3 63

Worksheet: Identifying Food Programming 64
From Diets to Foodways 67
   Experimenting with Foodways 68
   Worksheet: What Do You Want to Eat for? 69
What if Food is Not Something I Value? 70
How Do I Tell if I'm Hungry? 71
   Mechanistic Eating 71
References 73

8 Embodying Your Values — 74

Worksheet: Acceptance Practice #4 74
Embodying Your Values 74
Fashion without Self-Hatred: How? 76
   Values-Driven Self-Presentations 77
   Worksheet: My Values-Driven Self-Presentation 81
   The Bathing Suit Exercise 82
   Fashion Without Self-Hatred: Resources 82
   Surprising Your Mirror 83

9 Dancing with Your Body to the Life You Really Want — 85

Worksheet: Acceptance Practice #5 85
Dancing with Your Body to the Life You Really Want 85
Barriers to Your Values 87
   Worksheet: The Magic Wand Revisited 88
   Worksheet: My Hero 91
   Worksheet: My Barriers 93
The Magic Wand Revisited 94
   Worksheet: My Next Steps 95
Congratulations on Your Valued Life! 96

Index 97

Acknowledgments

Lots of wonderful people and organizations helped make this book a reality. My mentors, Mark Hegel, Jay Hull, and Steve Bartels, were all unbelievably generous with their time, wisdom, and humor; neither this book nor I myself would have developed as well without them. The Department of Psychiatry at the Geisel School of Medicine at Dartmouth provided the early funding without which *Accept Yourself!* could never have been developed. Alan Green, psychiatry department chair, championed this work from the beginning and I am deeply grateful. The Hitchcock Foundation generously awarded me a 2015 Hitchcock Foundation Scholars career development award that made the research and writing behind this book possible. I owe both Jennifer Reining and Karen Jones at the Foundation my gratitude. Stephanie Morton co-authored the original self-help workbook for the *Accept Yourself!* intervention; her ideas are suffused throughout this book. My patients and research participants shared their experiences with candor, and helped guide me to the most helpful experiences. Michelle Neyman Morris consulted helpfully on nutrition and health behavior change aspects of the program. My postdoctoral fellows, John Park, Evan Bick, and Monica Lindgren, all assisted with the research. Theresa Glaser, John Billig, and Linda Bacon gave important help developing treatment fidelity measures. My husband and son supported me while I wrote and worked late nights and weekends. Finally, *Accept Yourself!* was also supported by a Health Promotion and Disease Prevention Research Center supported by Cooperative Agreement Number U48DP005018 from the Centers for Disease Control and Prevention. The information and conclusions in this book are mine and do not necessarily represent the official position of the Centers for Disease Control and Prevention.

Introduction: Who This Book is for and How to Use it

If you hate your body and how you look, if you have tried and failed at various diets or other attempts to change it, if your body image makes you feel bad about yourself and contributes to depression or an unhealthy relationship with food, this book is for you. If you're frustrated and tired from trying strategies that don't work to feel good about your body, this book is for you. You may already know that you need a new path to wellness and self-acceptance. This book shows you that path. Inside this book you will find research, writings, and interactive exercises and experience that will help you understand why you haven't been able to successfully lose weight for good, and that will help you forgive yourself for that fact. You'll find out how to stop engaging in futile struggles with weight loss and body image, and you'll directly experience real acceptance and genuine well-being in the body you have now. You'll develop a new relationship with physical activity, food, and how you look that offers you adventure and joy instead of shame and guilt. Finally, you'll discover a powerful new path to achieve your dreams and goals now, without waiting another moment for your body and mind to change.

HOW TO USE THIS BOOK
This book isn't just a book; it's an experience. For this book to help you, you have to dive into it. Every chapter has new adventures for you, some quiet ones that you can do in bed with pencil and paper, and some dramatic, exciting, even scary ones that take place out in the real world. Some of the adventures will take you through some dark and difficult territory: You will be like Dorothy in the *Wizard of Oz*, who – if she wanted to get where she wanted to – had to walk a challenging path, meeting wonderful people, and having thrilling experiences, but also facing doubt, danger, loss, failure, and sadness along her way. But all of these experiences, both difficult and fun, will carry you closer to your destination, a life well lived, full of self-acceptance and the things that matter most to you. Also, as you write in and interact with the book, it will become a record of a turning point in your life; a time when you gave up on self-hatred and an unhelpful struggle with your mind and body, and began a life committed to your deepest wishes and dreams. For that to happen, your participation is required!

The book is organized into three parts: In Part 1, you'll explore your previous efforts at weight control and body-image change, and you'll also learn more about the research into how this process works for other people, and why it hasn't worked as well as you expected. In Part 2, you'll begin the process of achieving self-acceptance of your body, as well as a healthy relationship with food. You'll learn powerful emotional self-acceptance strategies that can be used with negative body image or any troubling emotion to more fully experience it and learn from it, using it as fuel to power you toward the life you want. Finally, in Part 3, you'll identify, experiment with, and commit to your values related to food, appearance, and life in general, tackling troublesome mental and practical barriers along the way. In this part of the book, a life rich with your values, wishes, and dreams will take shape, as you allow your body and mind to carry you to the life you want most.

I CAN NEVER ACCEPT MY BODY AT THIS WEIGHT: IS THIS BOOK RIGHT FOR ME?
This book is your adventure, and your opportunity to live in your body in a very different way than you may have considered before, so try it! The book itself will help guide you through a process to

help you discover if self-acceptance (and this book) is the right approach for you now, and it will help you identify better options if not. This approach isn't right for everyone. As you work through this introduction and Part 1, you'll learn if it's right for you.

One group of people who might not be helped enough by this book are people who have eating disorders. If you are concerned that you may have an eating disorder, but are not sure, the National Eating Disorders Association (NEDA) has an online screening tool that can help you decide if you might need professional help. The NEDA Screening Tool is available here: www.nationaleatingdisorders.org/screening-tool. If the NEDA Screening Tool suggests that you might have an eating disorder, you can use the website to help you locate psychologists, nutritionists, and physicians who can help. Eating disorders, regardless of your weight, can be life threatening, so it's important to get professional help if you might have an eating disorder. If you do have an eating disorder, this book might still help you develop a healthier relationship with food and your body. But you should use it with professional guidance and help.

A WORD ABOUT LANGUAGE

What do you call your body, when you look at it in the mirror? How do you describe it? In this book, we're going to learn a lot about the importance of language: how language can both help us and serve our goals, and also how language has a "dark side," where it can cause problems and harm. One goal of this book is to practice and experiment with using non-judgmental language around body image. Notice that I said "practice and experiment with," not "change," and also "non-judgmental language," not "non-judgmental thoughts." It is nearly impossible to change or control your thoughts. In fact, trying to get rid of an unpleasant thought generally makes it bigger and more stubborn! But the language we choose to use about our bodies, out loud, in front of others, and even quietly, to ourselves in the mirror, is open for experiment, and we can practice using unfamiliar words as we speak and see how those words impact us.

What does it mean to practice and experiment with using non-judgmental language about our bodies? One thing it means is to use non-judgmental language for body shape and size. For example, in this book, I *mostly* avoid using the words "obesity" or "obese" or "overweight." These words are *sometimes* used here, when discussing research findings or classifications based on Centers for Disease Control cutoffs for body mass index (BMI) classification (see Chapter 2), because that classification system uses these words to describe different weight and height combinations. However, apart from when I use these words to summarize research, they are not used in this text. Why not? The word "obesity" is problematic because it implies that this weight is in and of itself a problem, a disease state. The American Medical Association did, indeed, vote in 2013 to classify obesity as a disease, hoping to increase insurance company reimbursement for obesity treatments. However, it did so against the recommendation of its own Council on Science and Public Health, which it had commissioned to study the issue and make recommendations, and the decision to classify obesity as a disease remains controversial (Stoner & Cornwall, 2014). Many people who meet the current classification for obesity in terms of BMI are metabolically (and otherwise) healthy, so use of the word obesity to describe their body size is inappropriate. And for larger-bodied people who are not healthy, obesity is still an inappropriate word, because it implies their weight is the cause of their ill health, rather than their disease. Similarly, the word "overweight" implies that, for a given individual, there is a known, optimal weight for health, which that individual exceeds. As you will learn in Chapter 2, there is limited knowledge about what the optimal weight for health is for individuals.

In general, in this book, the words "fat" or "larger-bodied" are used to describe people with larger-than-average body sizes. Like "short," "tall," or "slender," "fat" can be a simple descriptive word to denote body type. However, it is also a stigmatized word that can be used, by itself, as a slur. There is a movement among size-acceptance activists to "take back" this word, just as lesbian, gay, bisexual, and transgender activists took back the word "queer," and I am in support of this effort. Therefore, the word "fat" is used frequently, and non-judgmentally, throughout the book. Fat is a body type, like tall or short, which can be referred to lightly, in passing, as you might describe your height. Because this word may have been used to hurt you in the past, you may not find this a non-judgmental word for your body, and that is fine. You do not have to use it! One possibility is "larger-bodied," which is another term used frequently in this book. Many people like words that represent positive judgments about larger body sizes, like "abundant," "plus-sized," or "curvy," and you might want to experiment with these words, especially if you usually use negatively judgmental words to describe your larger-than-average body. However, in this book, I avoid words that convey judgment of body size, whether positive or negative, because this program treats weight as a neutral (neither positive nor negative) human characteristic, and also because the use of euphemisms can imply judgment about the word ("fat") being avoided when we use them. If you are living in a larger-than-average body, I encourage you to try out "fat" or "larger-bodied" and see if you can reclaim these words or use them in a non-judgmental way, as well as practice using positive judgment words, like "abundant," to describe yourself and see what that is like. I encourage you to use these words even if your mind is still critical that you are "overweight."

What if you are struggling with body image, but are not living inside a larger-than-average body? People of all weights struggle with judgmental thoughts and language about their bodies. Women of all sizes call themselves and have been called by others "fat" as a slur. I use the phrase "average-weight" to describe body sizes that are close to the numerical mean for Americans, which is a BMI of 27 for both men and women. Words that denote larger-than-average body size, like "fat" or "larger-bodied," are obviously not accurate, non-judgmental language for average-weight individuals. So if you are close to the average weight, I encourage you to practice calling yourself "average weight," rather than another term. If you weigh somewhat or substantially less than average, you might experiment with calling yourself "thin" or "slender" as non-judgmental terms. If you are average-weight or less, it is especially important that you do not use words like "fat" or "large" to describe your body, even though these words may be appropriate non-judgmental language for a larger-than-average person. Because they are stigmatized words, when you use them inaccurately to describe yourself you are promoting and advocating both negative judgments about larger-than-average bodies, and also unrealistic weight and size standards for anyone who hears you. Your comments are offensive to larger-bodied people, because they imply that you, as an average-sized or smaller person, consider yourself unacceptable in size. And if you are unacceptable in size, by implication you criticize anyone larger than you. Using accurate, non-judgmental language, regardless of size, is an excellent beginning practice for self-acceptance.

What are some accurate, non-judgmental words you can use to describe your body? (Fat, larger-bodied, average-sized, thin?) Write them here and commit to practicing using them when you talk about your body. Don't worry about changing your judgmental thoughts. Just, when you catch yourself having such a thought, try using these words in addition and see how that feels. Also, try using these words publicly, to describe yourself or others.

INTRODUCTION

What are some positive-judgment words you can use to describe your body? (Curvaceous, curvy, zaftig, abundant, soft, attractive, pretty, beautiful?)

_____

_____

_____

_____

_____

_____

How do these words feel? You might try using these words occasionally, especially if you have never described your body in positive terms or heard it described that way. The goal in using these words is not to convince yourself that they are true or false. They are judgments. They are not factual. They are neither true nor false for anyone. Instead, the goal is simply to observe what using them as a practice feels like, and what other effects it has. I encourage you to practice mainly with non-judgmental words, rather than positive-judgment words, because your weight and shape are neutral facts about you, not a virtue or a vice. But experimenting with positive words is also worthwhile, to see what happens when you use these.

OK. You've got your book of adventures ready. You have a pencil handy, and you've already marked up the book. You have some words to use along the way. You are ready for an exciting journey! Let's begin.

REFERENCE

Stoner, L., & Cornwall, J. (2014). Did the American Medical Association make the correct decision classifying obesity as a disease? *The Australasian Medical Journal, 7*(11), 462–464.

PART 1

Your Weight, Your Body: Can You Control It? (And Why Not?)

1
Your Body Struggle: Evaluating Your Progress Thus Far

If you're reading these lines, chances are good you've spent some period of time – weeks? months? years? decades? – engaged in a struggle with your body. Chances are, this book is not the first thing you've tried to feel better about your weight, shape, and how you look. If this book has any hope of really changing your life and your relationship with food or your body, one thing we should avoid from the outset is repeating mistakes you've already made. So this chapter asks you to take a hard look at why these issues are a struggle for you, what you've already tried to solve them, and what that means for what you should try next. Many people feel overwhelmed or hopeless about solving their problems when they look at a long list of strategies that once gave them hope but didn't fulfill their promises, so don't be surprised if this chapter is painful or emotional for you to complete. But, by honestly evaluating what you have already tried and its effects, you may uncover a new path. The struggle that has engaged you has been painful. This book offers you a new and very different path towards your dreams. But first, let's examine the road you have already taken.

WHAT HAS YOUR STRUGGLE COST YOU?

One way to begin considering a problem is to name it, to come up with some word or phrase that captures exactly how you think about this problem. Susan, who had struggled with her weight and eating since childhood, experiencing bulimia nervosa, Overeaters Anonymous, Weight Watchers, fitness work with a personal trainer, a variety of diets and diet books, and finally two weight loss surgeries with weight loss and subsequent regain along the way, called her problem "being stuck." You may call it "my weight," or "my overeating," or "my fat," or something else. Take a moment, close your eyes, and dig down in your mind deeply, to the center of the problem. What is at the core? What do you call it? How do you name this problem? Write its name on the next page, at the top of the worksheet "What has this problem cost you?"

Now that this problem has a name, take a moment and consider all the ways this problem has cost you. How has it hurt you? What opportunities has it taken from your life? Has it cost you money? Relationships? Work? A positive self-image? Other good things in your life? List all the costs – everything it has taken from you. Don't leave anything out. (Feel free to add space on another page if this worksheet isn't enough.)

You may notice tears, rage, or anxiety emerging as you make your list. If that happens, welcome those feelings in. This problem may have cost you a lot. This is a place to mourn those losses in your life. Write everything down.

What Has This Problem Cost You?

The Problem: _____

Costs:

- _____
- _____
- _____
- _____
- _____
- _____
- _____
- _____
- _____
- _____
- _____
- _____
- _____
- _____
- _____
- _____
- _____
- _____
- _____
- _____
- _____
- _____
- _____
- _____
- _____

What was it like to make your list? Was it easy? Difficult? Was the problem more costly than you had imagined? Did you feel any emotions as you made your list? Many emotions are possible, from anger to rage to sadness to hopelessness to guilt and shame. These feelings can be quite intense, but, for now, just notice them and welcome them in. After all, they're there for a reason: As we'll talk about more later, we live in a culture that prizes physical appearance, and if your body has ever been in any way less than "perfect" in your own eyes, the eyes of people you care about, or even compared to people you see in the media, you may have paid a price. Perhaps even a very costly, painful price.

YOUR BODY OVER TIME

Looking at all the ways this problem has cost you may make you angry, sad, or ashamed: This problem has been painful. This problem has hurt you. But it may also leave you feeling determined: *This is why this problem has to change*. To have a good life, you may feel that you have to get rid of your problem, to solve it. Is this feeling familiar? Perhaps you've had these feelings – the anger, the sadness, the shame, the guilt, the fear, the determination about your body and your eating – before. In fact, these feelings may have hung around for a long time, along with lots of other positive and negative feelings and experiences in and with your body.

The Timeline Exercise (adapted from Heffner & Eifert, 2004) allows you to organize your history in your body in whatever way makes sense to you. It lets you capture in a visual format all of the important life events in your body history. On the next page, you'll see a simple timeline. The blanks along the bottom let you fill in dates, ages, whatever way you want to organize time. You can take the timeline up to the present, or project it into the future. It's up to you. In terms of what to put on the timeline, that's up to you, too, but it might include your weight or shape history, your dieting history, health events that affected you, and other events that affected your self-image. It should definitely include other important life experiences, positive and negative, that shaped who you are today. Some people like to put positive events above the line, and negative events below the line, but you can organize it however you would like, because it's your history. You might want to paste in photographs, write in comments, or personalize it in some other way.

Your Body Timeline

Reviewing your timeline, what do you notice? One thing you may notice is that body shape and weight don't take as big a role as you might have expected. Therapists Michelle Heffner and Georg Eifert (2004) have pointed out that despite using timelines like these for many years with women with anorexia, to whom achieving a goal weight is often extremely important, they had never seen a client list a weight-related achievement. Like their clients, you probably didn't write "reached 90 pounds!" or "fit into my skinny jeans!" as major achievements on your timeline. Instead, the events that are significant to you may reflect your values and passions, or your personal tragedies.

The struggle with weight and shape may also have appeared on your timeline, in the form of weight loss efforts, eating disorders, or negative weight-related comments or cruelty by others. Is this true for you? How do weight and shape struggles appear on your timeline? What does this mean to you?

Some people note their weight in various places on their timeline, and some don't. If you didn't, notice that: Most people do not, and that may be because deep down, the number on the scale doesn't matter as much to us as the experiences and life events we truly value. Some people do put in significant "numbers on the scale" in their struggle with weight. Notice that, again, this isn't because they are valued achievements. Sometimes the weights noted are linked to negative experiences – being weighed by doctors, family members, or for sports, and experiencing abuse from others related to the numbers on the scale. Another interesting thing about weight numbers, if they appear in your timeline, is to observe their pattern over time. For many people, seeing weight gain and increased body dissatisfaction over time is not unusual, but typical. Whether you charted in your weight numbers or not, consider: Is this true for you? Have you gained weight, lost weight, or stayed the same over time? What has happened to your body image over time? Has it gotten better, worse, or stayed about the same? Take a moment and jot down your answers to these questions, as well as any thoughts you have now about your body timeline.

_____

_____

_____

_____

_____

_____

WHAT HAVE YOU ALREADY TRIED TO SOLVE THIS PROBLEM?

Completing the timeline may have reminded you of some of the efforts you have tried to solve your problems with weight, shape, food, or body image. Considering these strategies is of essential importance, because an honest evaluation of what you have already tried and how well it has worked may point to solutions that worked well but have been abandoned prematurely, as well as steering you away from solutions that will not work no matter how hard you try to implement them. On the next page (and in a notebook, if you need more room), make a list of every single thing you have tried to solve the problem you have just named. Be exhaustive. Your list may include medications, therapies, surgeries, exercise programs, fashion changes, diets, self-talk or other attempts to change your thinking, gym memberships, personal trainers, food-delivery services, fasting, spa trips, eating or binging on "forbidden foods" in an effort to feel better, eating disordered behaviors, or any number of other strategies. List each strategy separately – each medication or diet pill by name, for example, each diet by name, and so on. The important thing is that you list every single thing you have tried to solve your problem, whether it was "healthy" or unhealthy, effective or not, helpful or not.

Once your list is complete, move to the second column, which asks you to consider how far each strategy has taken you. Be honest here. Did it help for a little while, but then stopped working? Did it make you feel better, without solving the problem? Did it make the problem worse? Did it work well, but you had to give it up? And if so, why? Was the strategy too costly in terms of money or time or effort? Was it dangerous or unhelpful in some other way? Don't say, "I was just lazy," or "It was my fault." A truly good strategy is one you will stick with, so for any seemingly helpful strategy that you gave up, honestly admit to the costs that made it hard to implement, rather than resorting to self-blame.

YOUR BODY STRUGGLE

What Strategies Have You Tried To Solve Your Problem?

- _____
- _____
- _____
- _____
- _____
- _____
- _____
- _____
- _____
- _____
- _____
- _____
- _____
- _____
- _____
- _____
- _____
- _____
- _____
- _____
- _____
- _____
- _____
- _____
- _____
- _____

How Far Has This Strategy Taken You Toward Solving Your Problem?

- _____
- _____
- _____
- _____
- _____
- _____
- _____
- _____
- _____
- _____
- _____
- _____
- _____
- _____
- _____
- _____
- _____
- _____
- _____
- _____
- _____
- _____
- _____
- _____
- _____
- _____

What do you notice as you look over your list? Is it comprehensive? Go back, and add in any last strategies you forgot, and evaluate each of them, too. How long is your list? Did you realize that you had worked this hard, or tried this many strategies, to solve this problem? When I do this exercise in therapy with my clients, I usually want to give them a gold medal for their hard work. Do you deserve a gold medal for your efforts to solve this problem? Even if the problem is still there, I think you do. You have worked hard, tried hard, and made an incredible, valiant effort to solve your problem with weight, shape, body image, and food. If you hate how you look, or you've received messages from other people that you should hate how you look, you may believe – or have been told – that your size and shape are your fault. But look at your list! Whatever size or shape you are: *It's not your fault.* You've given it your all – tried everything you can think of, and probably everything *I* can think of, too – and the problem remains.

What about your evaluations of these strategies? These are the most common evaluations I hear when I work with clients in therapy using this exercise:

1. The solution didn't work at all.
2. The solution made the problem worse.
3. The solution made me feel better, temporarily, but didn't actually do anything to solve the problem.
4. The solution worked temporarily, but the problem returned. (And sometimes, the problem returned and was even worse when it came back!)
5. The solution worked for some aspects of the problem, but didn't help with others (or made others worse).
6. The solution worked well, but I had to give it up because it was too costly or difficult to implement.
7. I am not sure whether this solution would work because I haven't given it a fair shot; I still think it may hold promise for solving the problem.

8. Other: _____

Take a moment and write in the numbers that correspond to how you've evaluated each strategy on your list. For example, perhaps you lost 30 pounds on the keto diet, and felt good about yourself and your body, but began to crave sugar so intensely that you binged, went off the diet, and regained 45 pounds. You might classify this as a number 4, or a number 6, or both.

Are there any number 7s, where you think a strategy still holds promise, but haven't yet given it a fair shot to work? If there are, the thing to do next is to put down this book, and pause. This book offers a truly different approach to your problem than any that are currently on your list, and I believe it is not worth your time to consider a new path if another well-worn strategy still holds promise for you. So if there are any strategies on your list that are truly 7s, go back to them and implement them until either (a) your problem is solved, or (b) they move into a different category on your list. Most people, considering these strategies honestly, realize that they *have* actually given the strategy a fair shot. It just didn't work, perhaps because it was too difficult or costly to implement. For example, if you did initially lose 30 pounds on a diet that you couldn't maintain, you might be tempted to ignore the evidence that it was too costly, and call that a number 7. If this is true for you, that strategy belongs in category 6, not 7. Be honest with yourself if you've tried a strategy but had to give it up because it was too costly. If it was too costly before, it is likely still too costly now.

Now that you've considered each of these strategies, I have one more set of questions for you about your problem. How old were you when your problem with weight, shape, food, or body image came into your life? _____ years old.

How old are you now? _____ years old.

How many years have passed since this problem entered your life? _____ years.

And since the problem entered into your life, when you were _____ years old, has the problem (circle one)…?

Gotten better

Gotten worse

Stayed about the same

Most of my clients say the problem has gotten worse or stayed the same. A (very) few say it has gotten a little bit better, but usually not by much, or not for long. What does this mean?

Looking back over the last few pages, this may be the pattern you see: You have worked hard, for many years, trying to solve your problem with weight, shape, body image, and food by every logical means that you had access to, and perhaps by every means you or anyone else could ever think of, regardless of danger or cost or likelihood of success. You have put in a good-faith effort. You have tried unbelievably hard. Nevertheless, despite this unrelenting effort to improve or solve the problem, here you sit, years later, with a bigger problem than you had when you started, or at least a problem that is no smaller or easier to solve.

Is that the case for you? How does that feel? For a lot of my clients, it feels hopeless. If we were sitting together, you might be looking at me wide-eyed right now, hoping that I have a solution that once and for all will fix this problem in a way none of your previous efforts ever has. Maybe this time, this program, this book will be the charm.

If that's the case, I have some terrible news for you. *I don't have the solution*. You've done everything I can think of, and probably many things I could never think of, to solve your problem with weight, shape, food, and body image, and yet the problem is still here, big as life and twice as distressing. I don't have any magic answer to control something that you, with all your best efforts, have been unable to control.

But what I can offer you is an image, which might help us at least understand the pattern you seem to be caught in. Take a moment and imagine a casino: The blackjack and craps tables, the slot machines. Your situation reminds me of this casino. When you go into a casino, go up to a slot machine, and insert a coin, what do you hope will happen? Certainly you hope that you will win! And if you take a roll of coins to the slot machine and play for a while, it is likely that you *will* win: a little bit, here and there, just enough, typically, that you may feel tempted to keep playing even after your initial budget is gone. Not only that, if you look around the casino, you will see posters and – if you're very lucky – flashing lights and clinking coins announcing that some people win, and win big. A tiny number of people go to a casino, win an enormous fortune, and, one hopes, never return. But what happens if you keep playing, roll after roll of quarters, for days, weeks, months on end?

You lose money. And the longer and harder and more faithfully you play, the more you lose, even though, as gambling addicts can tell you, from time to time you may be ahead, you may be winning. And why is this? Why is it that gambling addicts always lose money, even their entire fortunes, despite dedicated effort, over many years, in a place expressly designed to address their hopes to win big?

The reason is very simple: *Because the game is rigged*. The house will always win in the end, and the more money the gambling addict puts in, the more she will lose in the end. Could it be that the same is true for your game? Your dieting, weight loss, self-hatred game? Look back over your list and ask yourself if this is true: Did my problem ultimately get worse every time I tried to make it better? (And don't be like the gambler, who brags about his small wins without admitting to the much bigger losses – look at the net change for you over time in answering this question.) If the problem got worse every time you tried to make it better, then is possible that the solutions may be part of the problem? Take a moment and write down your thoughts about this question, and also today's date. Later, you may want to look back on how you felt about this idea before you began working through this book.

Today's Date: _____

_____
_____
_____
_____
_____
_____

REFERENCE

Heffner, M., & Eifert, G. H. (2004). *The anorexia workbook: How to accept yourself, heal your suffering, and reclaim your life*. Oakland, CA: New Harbinger Publications.

2
The Surprising Truth about Weight Loss

THE SCIENCE OF WEIGHT LOSS: IT'S NOT WHAT YOU THINK

If you feel like a failure in your efforts to change your body, lose weight, and achieve happiness, you are not alone. In fact, you are in excellent company. Most American women, and 40% of American men, report currently dieting or having dieted in the past year (Yaemsiri, Slining, & Agarwal1, 2011), and Americans spend about $60 billion – more than $180 for every man, woman, child, and infant – every year on weight loss products (Marketdata Enterprises, 2015). Researchers have also gotten in on the act: The National Institutes of Health spent $965 million on obesity research in 2016, more than it spent on ovarian cancer, lung cancer, and stroke combined.

But all that scientific, entrepreneurial, and ordinary human effort has not achieved much more than your own efforts have. If you have tried, and failed, to lose weight, *it is not your fault*. There is little evidence that *any* weight loss diet is strongly effective over the long term. In fact, as many as two-thirds of dieters in clinical trials *regain more weight than they lost* (Mann et al., 2007). The most effective clinical trials for non-surgical weight loss interventions find an average 3–6 percent long-term weight loss, and that is only using the most state-of-the-art interventions, and never discontinuing or taking a break from the weight loss strategy (Franz et al., 2007). In other words, if you weigh 200 lbs, and use the most effective weight loss, under optimal conditions, and continue them for the rest of your life, you can expect to lose an average of 6–12 lbs over the long term. If you plan to continue with weight loss, you should consider: Is that acceptable to you? Can you consider that amount a success, worth permanently continuing weight loss strategies (e.g., dieting or taking weight loss pills) to maintain? Even if the answer to that question is yes, you should be aware that weight loss outside of research settings is likely to be even more modest.

Indeed, these results are probably overestimates, because they are based on the randomized controlled trial literature. Clinical trialists only receive funding for interventions that show some initial promise, and clinical trials are conducted under ideal conditions, with motivated participants. Furthermore, unsuccessful trials are often not published. These factors mean that clinical research on weight loss probably underestimates the extent to which dieting is counterproductive. Research in non-laboratory situations offers additional evidence that dieting doesn't work. Among adolescent girls, self-reported dieting, exercise for weight control, and dietary restraint *actually predicts weight gain* and the onset of obesity, even among initially normal or underweight girls, a finding that has been replicated in several studies (Neumark-Sztainer, Wall, Haines, Story, & Eisenberg, 2007; Neumark-Sztainer, Wall, Story, & Standish, 2012; Stice, Cameron, Killen, Hayward, & Taylor, 1999).

If research suggests dieting causes weight gain, or at best, extremely modest weight loss, in most people, how do we explain people who do lose weight? You may know people who have lost significant weight, and you may have had periods of weight loss yourself. There is wide variation in people's response to weight loss, and a small minority of people are able to lose weight and keep it off. (You will know if you are in this select group if, in Chapter 1, your dieting history suggested that you were able to lose weight, keep it off permanently, and your problem was solved. Of course, if you were in this group, it is likely you would not have purchased this book.)

More importantly, however, most people are able to lose weight, even significant amounts of weight, temporarily. You may have lost significant weight multiple times. I have patients who report having lost *hundreds of pounds* on various diets and weight loss strategies over the course of their dieting histories. If this is you, you may feel terribly frustrated and ashamed. But weight loss followed by weight regain is the normal outcome of weight loss strategies, whether you keep using the strategy or not. In research, outcomes tend to be v-shaped or checkmark-shaped. Participants begin the weight loss effort, successfully lose weight, and then gradually regain it, until they are back to their baseline weight, just below it, or sometimes well above it, depending on how effective the strategy is. This happens even to people who stay on their diets or keep doing weight loss strategies. Weight regain isn't a result of poor willpower. It's the usual outcome. But why?

WHY MIGHT DIETING LEAD TO WEIGHT GAIN?

Our evolutionary ancestors coped with periods of feast and famine. For them, the ability to retain body weight and slow metabolism when starving was adaptive, and so was the ability to eat a lot, burn calories efficiently, and not change body shape and size dramatically in times of feast. If our ancestors had lost significant weight rapidly during periods of scarcity, they would not have survived to pass their genes on to us. Our bodies have features designed by evolution to cope with periods of feast and famine that make it difficult to deliberately lose weight.

Animals, when faced with caloric restriction or starvation, exhibit a host of biochemical, behavioral, and physiological changes designed to slow metabolism and more efficiently store available calories as fat in order to survive a long period of starvation (Wang, Hung, & Randall, 2006). In human beings, the body responds to loss of both fat mass and muscle mass with feedback signals that contribute to weight regain by changing how the body adapts to energy intake (Dulloo, Jacquet, Montani, & Schutz, 2015). Even if you adhere perfectly to your diet, these physiological changes still promote weight gain, as you may have personally experienced if you have lost weight and regained it. But the changes experienced by animals and human beings in response to calorie restriction are not only physical. They are behavioral (and in humans, psychological) as well.

You may think of times when you binged on high-fat or high-sugar foods during a diet as an example of loss of willpower or a psychological weakness. You might be surprised to learn that this behavior is one you share with other mammals. Laboratory rats who are exposed to intermittent calorie restriction or intermittent availability of palatable foods will increase eating (binge) when they have an opportunity, and they demonstrate a particular preference, under conditions of calorie restriction, for high-fat, high-sugar foods, such as cookies (Hagan & Moss, 1997). (Laboratory studies in rats in fact sometimes actually use Oreos.) This effect persists after the calorie restriction is removed and an otherwise normal diet is restored, and can lead to obesity in rats (Corwin, Aveeno, & Boggiano, 2011). If you have engaged in "stress eating" on a diet, it might surprise you even more to know that this effect of dietary restriction on rat food preferences and consumption is also increased by stress, such as exposure to foot shocks (Hagan et al., 2002).

Similar effects of calorie restriction occur in human beings as well. Consider the Minnesota Semi-Starvation Study (Keys, Brozek, Henschel, Mickelsen, & Taylor, 1950). Cardiologist Ancel Keys conducted research during World War II to establish the best methods for refeeding starving prisoners of war, and he subjected his participants to a six-month semi-starvation protocol as part of this research. The participants were young men who had registered as conscientious objectors to the war, and they were selected for the study because of their optimal physical and psychological health and hardiness. The semi-starvation protocol lasted six months, and was intended to cause participants to lose 25% of their body weight. Participants ate a 1,570-calorie-per-day diet, which might surprise you. Have you ever been on a diet (or even a post-diet "maintenance" eating plan) that prescribed fewer daily calories than that? If you have, and if you adhered to the diet for six months or more, you could expect to experience effects similar to what these young, semi-starved men experienced.

The effects of this diet on the men were profound. The men developed symptoms similar to women with eating disorders. They became obsessed with food, subscribing to food magazines, hoarding food if they had the opportunity, and developing unusual obsessive rituals around food consumption. They experienced severe emotional distress, including increased depression, emotionality, and physical health concerns, as well as fatigue, irritability, and decreased sex drive and sociability. They reported being less able to think and concentrate. One participant amputated three of his own fingers with an axe. Physically, in addition to weight loss, decreased strength and stamina, they also experienced decreased basal metabolic rate, with lower body temperature, respiration, and heart rate.

The results of the Minnesota Semi-Starvation Study raised serious ethical concerns about harming participants, and such studies are no longer done. Eating disorder researchers at the University of Minnesota followed up with Keys' participants 50 years later and discovered that many still had eating behavior changes (Crow & Eckert, 2000). If you have been on a similar diet for as long a time or longer, be aware that researchers would consider that unethical, and might expect you to experience long-lasting eating changes purely as a result of the biological effects of semi-starvation on your mind and body.

Our evolutionary legacy has designed us to respond strongly to lack of food. Dietary restraint (or starvation) leads to food cravings (particularly for fat, carbohydrates, and sugar), as well as loss of self-regulation over eating (binge eating), in order to protect us from harm. Viewed in this context, it makes sense that dieting behavior predicts overeating and weight gain (Polivy, 1996). Restrained eaters and dieters respond less than normal eaters to feeling full, and they respond more to the palatability or deliciousness of foods. Like the laboratory rats deprived of food and exposed to stress, dieters are more likely to show overeating in response to negative moods (Polivy & Herman, 1985).

The effects of hunger and deprivation on human beings are powerful, and cause people to eat more of high-calorie foods. This is a biological effect designed to prevent starvation, not a lack of willpower. Laboratory studies show that when dieters are given a high-calorie food, such as frosted cake, they tend to consume *more* of it than non-dieters. They also fail to regulate their consumption of high-calorie foods as non-dieters naturally do. For example, if non-dieters are presented cake twice in a row, they eat less of it the second time. Dieters, however, eat *more* cake on *both* occasions. (Polivy, 1996; Polivy & Herman, 1985). Dietary restriction *all by itself* sets people up to engage in binge behavior.

HOW BAD IS OBESITY FOR YOUR HEALTH?

But what about the effects of obesity on health? Most people believe that getting or staying thin is a prerequisite to a long, healthy life. Let's look at that idea a bit more closely. To do that, we start with your BMI (your body mass index). The BMI is a measure of body size that is less crude than a simple weight measurement in that it corrects for expected variation in weight due to height. Research done on obesity often uses BMI as its outcome measure. Before completing this quiz, it is helpful to know your own BMI. You can use the National Heart Lung and Blood Institute's online BMI calculator to find out yours here (ignore the weight loss discussion on their page): www.nhlbi.nih.gov/health/educational/lose_wt/BMI/bmicalc.htm. Write your BMI on the line below.

My BMI: _____

Now, which BMI category do you think has the highest mortality risk? Which has the lowest? In the blanks next to each category below, put a number to rank the categories in order from greatest to lowest risk of death. Use a "1" to indicate the highest risk, and a "5" for the lowest risk.

____ Underweight (BMI < 18.5)
____ Normal weight (BMI 18.5–24.9)
____ Overweight (BMI 25–29.9)
____ Obese (BMI 30–34.9)
____ Moderately/extremely obese (BMI > 35)

Now that you've guessed, here is the actual risk of mortality for each group across 30 years of follow-up, in order of *greatest* risk of death to least. These numbers are a summary of results across a series of large, representative, epidemiological studies done with US or Canadian samples, all of which have found the same rank ordering (Flegal, Kit, Orpana, & Graubard, 2013; Orpana et al., 2010; Strawbridge, Wallhagen, & Shema, 2000).

1. Underweight (BMI < 18.5) (RR = 1.38–2.31)
2. Moderately/extremely obese (BMI > 35) (RR = 1.32)
3. Normal weight (BMI 18.5–24.9) (RR = 1)
4. Obese (BMI 30–34.9) (RR = 1)
5. Overweight (BMI 25–29.9) (RR = 0.92)

RR means "relative risk," and the numbers on the right are summaries of the various large studies' findings of the relative risk of dying in various BMI categories. The researchers arbitrarily choose one category to compare the others against – in this case, that category is the normal-weight category. They arbitrarily assign the normal weight category a relative risk of 1. Then, you can compare the other categories' risk of death with the risk facing someone of normal weight. So, someone in the obese category is just slightly less likely to die than someone in the normal-weight category – they both have an RR of 1, but across studies the range suggests just a bit of an advantage for the obese people. The "overweight" category has a slightly smaller risk of death than the "normal" category. Folks who are underweight, however, are nearly twice as likely to die depending on the study as someone of normal weight – an RR of 2 means twice as likely, whereas an RR of 0.5 would mean half as likely to die as someone with an RR of 1.

As you can see, being overweight is associated, across a variety of studies, with decreased mortality compared with normal weight. Being *underweight*, however, is associated with the greatest risk of death of all of the groups.

How did your guesses compare to the actual results? Were you surprised? Was being obese less unhealthy than you imagined? In fact, you might be surprised to learn that being fat is associated some health benefits – such as protection from osteoporosis. Obesity is also less associated with disease for women, non-smokers, and older people relative to men, smokers, and younger people, so if you are female, a non-smoker, or older in age, and fat, you can feel even more reassured about the impact of your weight on your life expectancy. Furthermore, studies have shown that being fat appears protective and beneficial for individuals with certain diseases, especially as we age. Interestingly, although obesity is associated with increased risk of acquiring many chronic diseases, once you have a disease, obesity is often a protective factor promoting longevity and better health outcomes, a situation researchers call the "obesity paradox" (Lavie, McAuley, Church, Milani, & Blair, 2014). Obesity paradoxes – where obesity protects against mortality or morbidity from the disease – have been found for many diseases, including kidney disease, infections, cancer, lung disease, heart disease, osteoporosis, anemia, high blood pressure, rheumatoid arthritis, and type II diabetes. Fat can serve as a biological resource, helping us to survive longer and better with illness.

Even in situations where obesity is clearly associated with disease risk, rather than benefit, it is not clear that weight loss – even if it were possible – would eliminate that risk. It's not clear that the risk profile of someone who has successfully and intentionally lost weight resembles that of someone who was always lower weight. In fact, the health effects of successful weight loss are controversial. Some studies find that intentional weight loss is associated with increased, not decreased, mortality (Allison et al., 1999; Sørensen, 2003), and other studies, like the Diabetes Care in General Practice Study (Hansen, Siersma, Beck-Nielsen, & de Fine Olivarius, 2013; Køster-Rasmussen et al., 2016), find that intentional weight loss does not improve survival.

ARE THE HEALTH EFFECTS OF WEIGHT AFFECTED BY CULTURE AND DISCRIMINATION?

Some data suggest that it may be the experience of being discriminated against because of being fat or living in a culture that stigmatizes fat that causes some of the health problems associated with obesity. Weight *dissatisfaction* is a stronger predictor of physical health outcomes than BMI, and both within and across cultures, groups with lower fat stigma experience less obesity-associated disease mortality and morbidity (Muennig, Jia, Lee, & Lubetkin, 2008). Feeling negatively about your weight also relates to metabolic syndrome for people at all weights (Pearl et al., 2017), whereas weight stigma and discrimination help explain the relationship between BMI and self-reported physical health and quality of life (Hunger & Major, 2015; Latner, Barile, Durso, & O'Brien, 2014). Finally, there is increasing evidence that the stress of weight stigma also causes *weight gain* (Tomiyama, 2014). Some research also suggests that it is a cycle of gaining and losing weight – so called yo-yo dieting – that may cause some of the health problems associated with obesity (Montani, Schutz, & Dulloo, 2015).

REFERENCES

Allison, D. B., Zannolli, R., Faith, M. S., Heo, M., Pietrobelli, A., Vanltallie, T. B., ... & Heymsfield, S. B. (1999). Weight loss increases and fat loss decreases all-cause mortality rate: results from two independent cohort studies. *International Journal of Obesity, 23*(6), 603–611.

Corwin, R. L., Avena, N. M., & Boggiano, M. M. (2011). Feeding and reward: Perspectives from three rat models of binge eating. *Physiology and Behavior, 104*(1), 87–97.

Crow, S., & Eckert, E. D. (2000, April). *Follow-up of the Minnesota Semistarvation Study participants.* Paper presented at the Ninth International Conference on Eating Disorders, New York.

Dulloo, A. G., Jacquet, J., Montani, J. P., & Schutz, Y. (2015). How dieting makes the lean fatter: From a perspective of body composition autoregulation through adipostats and proteinstats awaiting discovery. *Obesity Reviews, 16*(S1), 25–35.

Flegal, K. M., Kit, B. K., Orpana, H., & Graubard, B. I. (2013). Association of all-cause mortality with overweight and obesity using standard body mass index categories: A systematic review and meta-analysis. *Journal of the American Medical Association, 309*(1), 71–82.

Franz, M. J., VanWormer, J. J., Crain, A. L., Boucher, J. L., Histon, T., Caplan, W., ... & Pronk, N. P. (2007). Weight-loss outcomes: A systematic review and meta-analysis of weight-loss clinical trials with a minimum 1-year follow-up. *Journal of the American Dietetic Association, 107*, 1755–1767.

Hagan, M. M., & Moss, D. E. (1997). Persistence of binge-eating patterns after a history of restriction with intermittent bouts of refeeding on palatable food in rats: Implications for bulimia nervosa. *International Journal of Eating Disorders, 22*(4), 411–420.

Hagan, M. M., Wauford, P. K., Chandler, P. C., Jarrett, L. A., Rybak, R. J., & Blackburn, K. (2002). A new animal model of binge eating: Key synergistic role of past caloric restriction and stress. *Physiology and Behavior, 77*(1), 45–54.

Hansen, L. J., Siersma, V., Beck-Nielsen, H., & de Fine Olivarius, N. (2013). Structured personal care of type 2 diabetes: A 19 year follow-up of the study Diabetes Care in General Practice (DCGP). *Diabetologia, 56*(6), 1243–1253.

Hunger, J. M., & Major, B. (2015). Weight stigma mediates the association between BMI and self-reported health. *Health Psychology, 34*(2), 172.

Keys, A., Brozek, J., Henschel, A., Mickelsen, O., & Taylor, H. L. (1950). *The biology of human starvation.* Minneapolis, MN: University of Minnesota Press.

Køster-Rasmussen, R., Simonsen, M. K., Siersma, V., Henriksen, J. E., Heitmann, B. L., & de Fine Olivarius, N. (2016). Intentional weight loss and longevity in overweight patients with type 2 diabetes: A population-based cohort study. *PLOS ONE, 11*(1), e0146889.

Latner, J. D., Barile, J. P., Durso, L. E., & O'Brien, K. S. (2014). Weight and health-related quality of life: The moderating role of weight discrimination and internalized weight bias. *Eating Behaviors, 15*(4), 586–590.

Lavie, C. J., McAuley, P. A., Church, T. S., Milani, R. V., & Blair, S. N. (2014). Obesity and cardiovascular diseases: implications regarding fitness, fatness, and severity in the obesity paradox. *Journal of the American College of Cardiology, 63*(14), 1345–1354.

Mann, T., Tomiyama, A.J., Westling, E., Lew, A.M., Samuels, B., & Chatman, J. (2007). Medicare's search for effective obesity treatments: Diets are not the answer. *American Psychologist, 62*, 220–233.

Marketdata Enterprises (2015). *The U.S. weight loss market: 2015 status report*. (Report No. FS50). Tampa, FL: Marketdata Enterprises.

Montani, J. P., Schutz, Y., & Dulloo, A. G. (2015). Dieting and weight cycling as risk factors for cardiometabolic diseases: Who is really at risk? *Obesity Reviews, 16*(S1), 7–18.

Muennig, P., Jia, H., Lee, R., & Lubetkin, E. (2008). I think therefore I am: Perceived ideal weight as a determinant of health. *American Journal of Public Health, 98*(3), 501.

Neumark-Sztainer, D., Wall, M., Haines, J., Story, M., & Eisenberg, M.E. (2007). Why does dieting predict weight gain in adolescents? Findings from project EAT-II: A 5-year longitudinal study. *Journal of the American Dietetic Association, 107*(3), 448–455.

Neumark-Sztainer, D., Wall, M., Story, M., & Standish, A. R. (2012). Dieting and unhealthy weight control behaviors during adolescence: Associations with 10-year changes in body mass index. *Journal of Adolescent Health, 50*(1), 80–86.

Orpana, H. M., Berthelot, J. M., Kaplan, M. S., Feeny, D. H., McFarland, B., & Ross, N. A. (2010). BMI and mortality: results from a national longitudinal study of Canadian adults. *Obesity, 18*(1), 214–218.

Pearl, R. L., Wadden, T. A., Hopkins, C. M., Shaw, J. A., Hayes, M. R., Bakizada, Z. M., ... & Alamuddin, N. (2017). Association between weight bias internalization and metabolic syndrome among treatment-seeking individuals with obesity. *Obesity, 25*(2), 317–322.

Polivy, J. (1996). Psychological consequences of food restriction. *Journal of the American Dietetic Association, 96*(6), 589–592.

Polivy, J., & Herman, C. P. (1985). Dieting and binging: A causal analysis. *American Psychologist, 40*(2), 193.

Stice, E., Cameron, R.P., Killen, J.D., Hayward, C., & Taylor, C.B. (1999). Naturalistic weight-reduction efforts prospectively predict growth in relative weight and onset of obesity among female adolescents. *Journal of Consulting and Clinical Psychology, 67*, 967–974.

Sørensen, T.I.A. (2003). Weight loss causes increased mortality: Pros. *Obesity Reviews, 4*(1), 3–7.

Strawbridge, W. J., Wallhagen, M. I., & Shema, S. J. (2000). New NHLBI clinical guidelines for obesity and overweight: will they promote health? *American Journal of Public Health, 90*(3), 340–343.

Tomiyama, A. J. (2014). Weight stigma is stressful. A review of evidence for the Cyclic Obesity/Weight-Based Stigma model. *Appetite, 82*, 8–15.

Wang, T., Hung, C. & Randall, D. (2006). The comparative physiology of food deprivation: From feast to famine. *Annual Review of Physiology, 68*, 223–251.

Yaemsiri, S., Slining, M. M., & Agarwal, S. K. (2011). Perceived weight status, overweight diagnosis, and weight control among US adults: The NHANES 2003–2008 Study. *International Journal of Obesity, 35*(8), 1063–1070.

3
The Magic Wand

Imagine you have a magic wand that really will give you the body and mind you have always dreamed of having. Your mental and physical health are both excellent. Your body looks and works exactly as you have always wished. Not only that, your body and mind will remain in this ideal state permanently, no matter what you eat, do, don't do, or how many years pass. What would your life be like? What would you do differently? Would you eat differently, knowing you had the ideal body and always would, and would never "need" to diet again? Are there different activities you would do in your fantasy body? Would your work be different? Your relationships? Your friendships? Your leisure activities? Would your clothing be different? Would your daily routine change? Write lots of details, and spend some time with this activity. Really be bold, and write down your biggest fantasies of life in your ideal mind and body. We will be coming back to this magic wand fantasy many times in future chapters.

MY MAGIC WAND FANTASY

_____
_____
_____
_____
_____
_____
_____
_____
_____
_____

Body acceptance blogger Kate Harding wrote an essay where she describes the "fantasy of being thin." (You can read her essay here: https://kateharding.net/2007/11/27/the-fantasy-of-being-thin) She notes that many women imagine undergoing profound changes in every aspect of their lives when they finally successfully lose weight. Looking over your magic wand fantasy: Is this true for you?

In fact, it's worth observing that if it weren't for this fantasy, you might not ever seek weight loss at all. You have perhaps realized now that weight loss strategies have not worked for you in helping you reach your fantasy. You've read the research that helps you understand that you are not alone, and that this is not your failure, but is, in fact, the failure of the entire weight loss industry. It hasn't worked because it *can't* work. If we imagine your fantasy as a castle on a distant hill, and weight loss is the road you were told to take to get to the castle, then the bad news is: That road is closed.

The good news is: There's another road to your castle on the hill, a much more direct and scenic route that will take you closer to your fantasy, not further away as weight loss may have done. That is the road that we will be taking in the rest of this book, and it can be explained in one sentence: *Pursue this fantasy life directly, without waiting for your body to change first.* Having the life you have always imagined, in the body you will have anyway, is the main goal of this book and treatment program. If you described your magic wand fantasy up above, you already have your road map and compass; the rest of the book is just a traveler's guide on your way.

Let's take a closer look at your road map. Magic wand fantasies often include some big (or small) dreams or goals. Gabriela wanted to look good in photographs. Nora wanted to visit the Havasupai Reservation in the Grand Canyon, which is famous for its waterfalls, but accessible only by a multi-day hike into the Canyon. Lee wanted to date and have sex. Chris wanted to feel confident and attractive. Tanisha wanted to get married and have children. Samia wanted to become a television news anchor. Jamie wanted a promotion at work. Tory wanted to go kayaking and hiking in the mountains. Chi wanted to dance in nightclubs. Aisha wanted to go back to school. You might think of these dreams as points on a map, destinations you'd like to reach (sometimes literally, in Nora and Tory's cases). The thing about dreams, about destinations in general, is that they have a black and white quality to them. Either you attain them, or you don't. Aisha will go back to school, or she won't. Tanisha will get married and have children, or maybe she won't. The destination you planned to visit will be reachable, or it won't. And what will you do then?

In plotting a journey, points on a map are not enough, especially when plans change and the destination is inaccessible or no longer there. You may find yourself out in the wilderness, miles from anything familiar, no cell phone signal. How do you navigate then? Perhaps you could use a compass. If dreams are the destinations on your map, *values* are your compass headings. What are values? Values are aspects of life that are important to you. Dreams generally have values underlying them, although you might have to do a little investigation to determine what values underlie your dreams. (Sometimes, two people will share the same dream, but with very different underlying values!)

For example, both Annette and Alejandra included on their magic wand fantasies "going sea kayaking." But asking both women about why they wanted this dream helped clarify their different values. Annette was picturing a sea kayaking adventure alone in the Pacific Northwest, seeing whales and starfish and bears. She had not pursued this dream because she worried that her body was not fit and healthy enough to manage the challenge safely. She also feared discrimination based on her body size from trip outfitters, and the stress of asking for a seat-belt extender on the plane flight. For Annette, the values underlying her dream of a sea kayaking trip were *pleasure* and *adventure*. Alejandra, however, wanted to go sea kayaking in Georgia, near her home. Her girlfriend was an avid sea kayaker, and had begged Alejandra to join her on her weekend trips with her kayaking club. Alejandra wanted to spend time with her girlfriend, but she had been worried that she would not fit into the kayaks the club used and would embarrass herself and her girlfriend by being unable to get into or out of the boat in front of her girlfriend's buddies. For Alejandra, the values underlying her dream of sea kayaking were expressing *love* and *closeness* in her relationship.

You can often identify a value underlying your dream by asking yourself *why* the dream is important to you, and what about it is important. The intriguing thing about values is that, unlike dreams, they are not ever finally reachable. They are not destinations on a map that you reach or fail to reach. Instead, like compass headings, you can always head in the direction of your values, regardless of whether or not you reach any given destination. For example, if Annette achieves her dream of kayaking alone in British Columbia, can she still pursue pleasure and adventure, or has she finished with pleasure and adventure in her life? Of course, she can still pursue pleasure and adventure. In fact, she may be so excited by her wonderful trip that she plans many more and larger adventures. At the same time, imagine Alejandra does not get to go sea kayaking with her girlfriend. In fact, her girlfriend breaks up with her, and Alejandra is badly hurt. She no longer needs or has the opportunity to go sea kayaking to express her love and closeness. She may feel unloved, hurt, and lonely. But can she still express love and closeness to others? Yes, even at this painful and dark time in her life, she can still find ways to express her values of love and closeness. Perhaps she makes the effort to attend her niece's quinceanera, and to bring a handmade gift she knows her niece and sister will love, even though she is sad and doesn't feel like going at all. Whether we are hitting the peak destinations or traveling through the dark valleys and feeling lost, our values are compass headings that guide us in the right direction.

Take a moment now and identify your dreams and values. On the next page, you'll find space to make a list of all the things you've dreamed of doing in your life, big and small. Many of them might be on your magic wand fantasy. Imagine you not only had the body and mind you've always wanted, but also had won the lottery, received all the necessary support, and that all the other barriers to achieving your dreams were eliminated. Dream big! What would you want if the sky were the limit? When your list is complete, in the next column, consider why each dream is important to you. What about it do you value? What aspect of it would still be important to pursue, even if the specific dream were not possible?

Your Dreams	Values (Why Is This important?)

Now that you've considered your dreams and values, on the next page, you will find your own dream map. You've seen pirate treasure maps, where X marks the spot where all the best things are hidden. Your map has multiple Xs to mark the spots that represent your dreams. Fill in the dreams from your magic wand fantasy and any others you would like to add. You can even create your own additional Xs on the map. If you'd rather, you could draw or paint your own dream map in a journal or to hang up.

Notice that there are also swamps and mountainous passes on your map. As you pursue your dreams – or even just daydream about them – you have probably already noticed that many problems arise. For Annette, when she daydreamed or read articles about sea kayaking the Pacific Northwest, she thought of flight attendants humiliating her during her plane flight, and getting lost or stuck on her journey because she had misjudged her strength or fitness. She also had called one outfitter, who had been rude and dismissive, insisting they could not accommodate her, when she asked if women her size were welcome. These experiences – the thoughts about the flight attendants, the thoughts about getting lost, and the experience of discrimination, are all barriers on her journey. They are the swamps where she gets stuck, or the mountain passes she has to navigate and climb. You'll find spots on your map to write in your barriers. These could be external barriers, such as not having enough money, experiences of discrimination, not knowing anyone to date, having been rejected from your favorite school, or any other outside force that prevents you from reaching your dreams (or makes it more difficult to reach them). They could also be internal barriers – thoughts, feelings, fears that stop you from pursuing your dreams, even though no external forces have emerged to get in your way. Everyone, when they head out in the direction of their values to pursue their dreams, runs into both internal and external barriers. There are likely to be many of these on your journey. Some of the barriers you imagine as serious problems now may turn out to be no big deal. Other barriers may emerge that you haven't even imagined. For now, though, fill in the barriers that stop you on the map. Label the treacherous passes and mucky swamps with barriers that seem to stand in your way, and again, feel free to add more if you like. You can add a sea monster or two, if you'd like, carrying especially scary or serious barriers.

Finally you'll notice there's a compass rose, to help you keep your bearings. Label the points on the rose with your values, the reasons why you are pursuing your dreams. For Alejandra, after her breakup, she identified her dreams as including: having a happy marriage and children, writing children's books, volunteering in the children's ministry at her church, and having a beautiful home. Barriers included not having a dating partner, fears that as a fat woman she would not be able to attract a quality partner, bad experiences with online dating, fears that her art was not good enough to sell books, lack of time, and lack of money. She labeled her values (compass headings, why these dreams are important) as: Expressing Love, Being Close, Helping Children, Art, Beauty, and Catholicism/Spirituality.

So now you have your map. You've considered how your life would be different if a magic wand could take your body and mind struggles away. You've identified your dreams, values, and some of the barriers that stand in the way. You know where you want to go, and the kind of life you've always imagined. Having that life – in the body you have now – is the main goal of the remainder of this book. To get there, we will use your map and compass headings as a guide, and we will also learn some special skills to make the journey more effective. In the rest of this book, you'll learn how to see your body and hear your negative "body talk" without buying into negative self-judgments as the literal truth, and without behaving based on weight control strategies that haven't worked for you. You will practice developing self-acceptance. Finally, you'll use these developing skills – and your map – to identify how you want to eat, move, and live towards your dreams, successfully navigating the internal and external barriers that emerge along the way.

In the meantime, however, you may have your doubts. Particularly if you have (or fear) a physical health problem that is often tied to weight or weight loss, you may wonder, "how can I pursue the magic wand fantasy of good health," without engaging in weight loss? Will working on self-acceptance of your current body harm your efforts to make health changes and avoid disease?

Dreams and Values Map

BARRIER MTNS
SWAMP

IS *ACCEPT YOURSELF!* RIGHT FOR ME IF I HAVE TO DIET FOR MY HEALTH?
What if you have a medical condition for which weight loss has been suggested? What if you are worried about developing a medical problem because of your weight? What if you are trying to lose weight for your health? Is *Accept Yourself!* still right for you? What about your health?

Although obesity is a risk factor for some diseases, including cardiovascular disease, type II diabetes, hypertension, obstructive sleep apnea, and some cancers (Lavie, McAuley, Church, Milani, & Blair, 2014), health is individualized *and is not perfectly correlated with body size*. People *of all sizes* have high cholesterol, diabetes, heart disease, and hypertension. Many fat people are in excellent health. There are nearly 20 million metabolically healthy obese individuals in the US. (Wildman et al., 2008). A fat body is not, in and of itself, an unhealthy body, and you cannot tell someone's health status just by looking at them. If you are in good health, that is fortunate for you!

However, even if your health is poor, it is important to understand that most diseases associated with obesity have a large genetic component, and obesity may be the outcome, not the cause, of the disease process. Good or poor health is not fully controllable by anyone, and is not your fault. In addition, even if excess adipose tissue were the cause of your disease, as we discussed in Chapter 2, we do not currently have effective treatment to change your weight, and weight cycling (also called yo-yo dieting) is itself a risk-factor for chronic diseases, such as cardiovascular disease (Montani, Schutz, & Dulloo, 2015). Some research suggests that the best outcomes for people with chronic diseases such as diabetes occur for people who maintain their weight (rather than losing weight; Hansen, Siersma, Beck-Nielsen, & de Fine Olivarius et al., 2013).

A Health At Every Size® Approach to Health
If you have been told that your weight is to blame for your health problems, you may have trouble imagining how you could ever be healthy at your current weight. In fact, research suggests that making positive health changes is beneficial, regardless of weight. According to one large, nationally representative study that observed participants for an average of 14 years, there were no mortality differences between obese, overweight, and normal-weight individuals if they regularly engaged in two or more of these four health behaviors: Eating at least five servings of fruits and vegetables daily, exercising more than 12 times per month, consuming alcohol in moderation (or less), and refraining from smoking. Also, the more of these behaviors a person did, the longer the lifespan, regardless of weight (Matheson, King, & Everett, 2012).

This book takes an approach to physical health that is known as Health At Every Size®. Health At Every Size (HAES) is a trademark of the Association for Size Diversity and Health (ASDAH), which is an organization of health professionals who promote this approach. You can visit the ASDAH website to learn more at www.sizediversityandhealth.org.

These are the HAES principles:

1. Weight Inclusivity: Accept and respect the inherent diversity of body shapes and sizes and reject the idealizing or pathologizing of specific weights.
2. Health Enhancement: Support health policies that improve and equalize access to information and services, and personal practices that improve human well-being, including attention to individual physical, economic, social, spiritual, emotional, and other needs.
3. Respectful Care: Acknowledge our biases, and work to end weight discrimination, weight stigma, and weight bias. Provide information and services from an understanding that socio-economic status, race, gender, sexual orientation, age, and other identities impact weight stigma, and support environments that address these inequities.
4. Eating for Well-being: Promote flexible, individualized eating based on hunger, satiety, nutritional needs, and pleasure, rather than any externally regulated eating plan focused on weight control.
5. Life-Enhancing Movement: Support physical activities that allow people of all sizes, abilities, and interests to engage in enjoyable movement, to the degree that they choose.

We will use these principles throughout this book to improve health and well-being, and we will use them today to explore and respond to your physical health.

Making Health Changes

There *are* some things you can do – apart from weight control – to optimize your physical health. One of the most important is receiving regular medical care from a health provider you trust, including appropriate screening for diseases. For many fat people, fear of being stigmatized for their weight, as well as experiences of weight-based abuse and discrimination, prevent them from accessing needed medical care. Fat people get less preventative care and fewer cancer screenings, because of weight-based stigma (Phelan et al., 2015). It is not difficult to see how obesity would be a risk factor for poor health if discrimination prevents fat people from getting good medical care! In later chapters, we will discuss how to cope with discrimination in health care, but, for now, just know that you have the right to health care that does not shame you or make you feel bad about your weight or shape. If you have been avoiding medical care, now might be an excellent time to go to a doctor and get some information about your health. If you cannot find a doctor who treats you respectfully and without weight-based stigma, you can look for a new provider using ASDAH's "find a provider" tool online at: www.sizediversityandhealth.org/content.asp?id=32.

If it's impossible to find a respectful, non-stigmatizing doctor, it still may be worth a visit to obtain medical information. Reminding yourself that you deserve excellent care at any size, labeling the doctor's behavior as inappropriate and unprofessional, whether out loud or only in your own mind, and providing yourself with a reward and self-compassion for going to the appointment all may help. Make an effort, one way or another, to obtain some basic screening information about your health. Some common test results you might find helpful in monitoring your health apart from weight are listed below; ask your doctor for this information (or obtain these tests in another way, such as through a drugstore health clinic) and record the results here. With this information in hand, you will be able to make some simple choices about what health changes (if any) to make, and you will also be able to check back on your progress over time and see if they are helpful.

My Health Screening Results (at the Beginning of *Accept Yourself*!)

Today's Date: _____/_____/_____

My Blood Pressure: _____(systolic)/_____(diastolic)

Fasting Blood Glucose: _____mg/dL

Total Cholesterol:_____ mg/dL

LDL Cholesterol:_____ mg/dL

HDL Cholesterol:_____ mg/dL

Triglycerides:_____ mg/dL

Cholesterol Ratio: _____

Treatment guidelines and test result interpretation for these tests vary substantially over time, are complex, and should be individualized, so your doctor is the best person to tell you what these test results mean for you, as well as to make recommendations about what to do about these results.

If you have any test results that your doctor thinks are elevated or abnormal, ask your doctor to make a list for you of health changes – *apart from weight loss* – that you can make to help your health screening numbers and your health improve. Ask your doctor to give you a list of *at least* five changes you could make to improve your health, and to prioritize them for you in order from most to least important. Have your doctor write the list down (or write it down yourself in the doctor's office). If your doctor insists on putting weight loss on the list, remind yourself that you can and will be ignoring that recommendation, since you have already learned that weight loss efforts are not helpful for you and your health. You'll find space for a list of doctor-recommended possible health changes. Remember, you don't have to (and probably can't) implement all of these recommendations.

My Doctor and I Brainstormed a List of Health Behaviors to Address My Health Concerns

Concern I am addressing with these changes: _____

Current test results relevant to this concern:

_____

_____

_____

_____

_____

Possible health changes that may help (NO WEIGHT LOSS):

1.

2.

3.

4.

5.

It's possible that, depending on your risk factors and diseases, your doctor recommended making specific dietary changes. You may have been told to lose weight so many times that you have lost sight of other health reasons for making dietary choices. What you eat may not matter for weight loss, but it may matter for good health. A "healthy diet" is varied, and is different for everyone. Learning what is healthy for you involves *both* using guidelines tailored to your specific health concerns (e.g., if you have hypertension, reducing sodium) and paying attention to how the foods you eat affect you, physically, emotionally, and in terms of taste and enjoyment. These dietary changes may improve your health. However, it's important to note that these changes will probably not make you lose weight.

If you've bravely met with your doctor, navigated any size discrimination or inappropriate behavior from your doctor's office, or in some other way gotten your health screenings done and brainstormed a list of possible health changes to make if you have any health concerns, you've done a great job so far exploring your physical health beyond your weight. What does all this mean? If your test results are normal, congratulations! Enjoy your good health. (And feel free to let any others who stigmatize you for your "unhealthy" weight know that you are in excellent health, if that feels good.)

If you had any elevated readings, finding a respectful, non-stigmatizing physician may be your top priority. Making lifestyle changes is unlikely to help you over the long run as much as consistent medical care. Besides finding a physician, however, for any elevated readings you discovered, you may want to pick one (yes, only one) small lifestyle change that you would like to make during the *Accept Yourself!* program to promote your health.

However, if you had no elevated readings, I want you to *skip* this step. Making "healthy" changes when you are not actually unhealthy may represent an unhelpful return to dieting strategies that have not helped in the past. Our focus here is on making one health change to address a specific health problem. Similarly, don't write "eat healthier," or even "eat more fruits and vegetables," unless that is a specific recommendation for the health problem you actually have.

One Health Change

Now it's time to choose one important change you would like to make. To help you change, a goal needs to be important, but it should also be specific and measurable. For example, if you have blood pressure in the pre-hypertensive range, you may choose to exercise more. But deciding to exercise by jogging 15 minutes five days a week is a better change goal than "exercising more," because it is specific and measurable. When your goal is specific and measurable, it is easier to track whether or not you have achieved it.

Here are some more examples of important, specific, measurable goals to address specific health concerns:

- From a woman with pre-hypertension: I will jog 15 minutes five days a week.
- From a woman with high triglycerides: I will contact my state's tobacco quit line to get free nicotine patches and access to a free health coach, get rid of my cigarettes, and quit smoking on February 22, 2019.
- From a woman with low HDL (high-density lipoprotein) cholesterol: I will take a Zumba class twice a week and take a brisk walk with my friend four times a week this winter.
- From a woman with high LDL (low-density lipoprotein) cholesterol: I will replace my butter with olive oil in cooking and on bread for three weeks and notice how this feels and tastes.
- From a woman with diabetes: For two weeks I will take my blood glucose levels before and two hours after eating, and keep a food diary where I write down what I eat, how I felt physically and mentally before and after eating, and what my results were, so I can learn more about how foods affect me.

If you had any elevated health readings on your screening tests, and you are interested in finding out if lifestyle changes can improve your health, choose *one* (just one!) change goal that is specifically relevant to your health problem. Write this goal on the line below. Remember, you should choose just *one* change, so try to make it important, specific, and measurable. Remember that the goal here is to improve your specific, personalized physical health risk factors. The goal is not to lose weight, so do not choose that as your health change goal. Also, if you had no elevated readings on your screening tests, congratulations! You do not need to write a health goal now.

My Health Change Goal (for Readers with a Specific Health Concern *Only*)

_____
_____

To find out whether this change helps your health, you should implement this change for one month. If you selected a dietary change, you should know that tastebuds regenerate every three weeks, so for the first three weeks this change may not feel "right" to you, or you may crave whatever flavors are missing from the change you made. Wait four weeks, then reassess. (You'll find a spot in upcoming pages to record whether you noticed any changes after your one month change.)

Take a moment and take some notes here about how and when you will implement your change. Do you need any materials, supplies, or special foods? When can you get them? Is there someone whose help you will need? When can you contact them? Note when and where and how you will be implementing your health change here.

Health Change Goals and Barriers

Making health changes can be very difficult, even if you have chosen an important, specific, and measurable goal. There are many barriers to implementing even an important change. Make note of the barriers and strategies you came up with here.

Possible Barriers To My Goal	Strategies To Overcome Barriers

Bookmark This Page!

Finally, bookmark this page. Come back to this page first in one month, and, second, when you are finished with this book. During these check-ins, these pages will help you evaluate the health change you made.

One-Month Bookmark Check-In

Today's Date: ____/____/____

Did you make a dietary change? If you did, try a taste of a food you cut out or happened to eat less of now that it's been four weeks. Your tastebuds have regenerated. Does it taste different? Do the foods you have changed to eating taste different to you after four weeks? Record what you notice here:

_____

_____

_____

_____

_____

How does your body feel after one month of making your health change? Do you notice any changes in your body, such as less constipation, better digestion, mood improvements, steadier energy levels, or other changes? Record any changes you noticed here:

_____

_____

_____

_____

YOUR WEIGHT, YOUR BODY

End-of-Book Check-In
Return to this bookmark when you have finished the *Accept Yourself!* program, and have your health risk factors checked again and record them here.

My Health Screening Results (at the End of *Accept Yourself!*)
Do not fill out this page until you have finished the rest of the book.

Post Program Date: _____/_____/_____

My Blood Pressure: _____(systolic)/_____(diastolic)

Fasting Blood Glucose: _____mg/dL

Total Cholesterol:_____ mg/dL

LDL Cholesterol:_____ mg/dL

HDL Cholesterol:_____ mg/dL

Triglycerides:_____ mg/dL

Cholesterol Ratio: _____

Did your results change at all based on the change you made? Record any changes you noticed (or if there were no changes) here.

_____

_____

_____

_____

If there were no changes, consider if there is a different life change you'd like to experiment with. Or, it is worth considering: Perhaps this health factor is not actually under your control. That is also useful information. Health is not the result of a simple addition of our own behaviors. Many health factors are beyond our control. Experimenting with making changes will tell you what makes difference and what doesn't.

REFERENCES

Hansen, L. J., Siersma, V., Beck-Nielsen, H., & de Fine Olivarius, N. (2013). Structured personal care of type 2 diabetes: A 19 year follow-up of the study Diabetes Care in General Practice (DCGP). *Diabetologia, 56*(6), 1243–1253.

Lavie, C. J., McAuley, P. A., Church, T. S., Milani, R. V., & Blair, S. N. (2014). Obesity and cardiovascular diseases: implications regarding fitness, fatness, and severity in the obesity paradox. *Journal of the American College of Cardiology, 63*(14), 1345–1354.

Matheson, E. M., King, D. E., & Everett, C. J. (2012). Healthy lifestyle habits and mortality in overweight and obese individuals. *The Journal of the American Board of Family Medicine, 25*(1), 9–15.

Montani, J. P., Schutz, Y., & Dulloo, A. G. (2015). Dieting and weight cycling as risk factors for cardiometabolic diseases: Who is really at risk?. *Obesity Reviews, 16*(S1), 7–18.

Phelan, S. M., Burgess, D. J., Yeazel, M. W., Hellerstedt, W. L., Griffin, J. M., & Ryn, M. (2015). Impact of weight bias and stigma on quality of care and outcomes for patients with obesity. *Obesity Reviews, 16*(4), 319–326.

Wildman, R. P., Muntner, P., Reynolds, K., McGinn, A. P., Rajpathak, S., Wylie-Rosett, J., & Sowers, M. R. (2008). The obese without cardiometabolic risk factor clustering and the normal weight with cardiometabolic risk factor clustering: Prevalence ation (NHANES 1999–2004). *Archives of Internal Medicine, 168*(15), 1617–1624.

PART 2
Body Acceptance

Congratulations. You have completed the first phase of the book. You've explored your history with your weight and shape problem, and you may now understand better why your efforts to improve your body and self-image have not worked out the way you expected or planned. You've had a chance to consider what your life would be like without this problem, and to begin making some life changes to support your body just as it is right now. Many people at this point understand that weight loss and body struggle haven't worked, but still find it difficult to give them up, because it is difficult to imagine how they could ever accept the body they have now. If that is your experience, I invite you to notice that thought, and welcome it along with you on the next part of your journey. Part 2 of this book focuses on developing body acceptance. Body acceptance is an active, exciting, sometimes frightening experience, not a set of thoughts you have to agree to or believe. It begins by noticing the thoughts and feelings and experiences you are already having about your body, and also coming to notice how you came to have those thoughts, feelings, and experiences. Let's begin!

4
Turning Down Programming, Tuning in to Your Body

Have you ever noticed that your negative thoughts about your body or yourself are not really your own? Notice that most of the personal, private thoughts people describe having about their bodies – "I'm fat and disgusting," "I've let myself go," "My body is gross," "I'm so overweight," "My body can't be healthy," "My obesity caused my diabetes" – are very similar. When we deliver the *Accept Yourself!* program in groups, the negative thoughts women disclose about themselves and their bodies are often much the same, even though the women are different from group to group. You may feel strongly that you are, for example, "fat and disgusting." (Or that the fatness on your body is inherently disgusting.) But have you ever noticed? You did not make up that idea. That is not a creative, original idea you invented yourself. So consider: When, where, and how did body shape, weight, and appearance become so important to you? Also consider: What did you learn, growing up, about how to manage emotions?

_____
_____
_____
_____
_____

These messages you were taught and still carry and abide by: Do you agree with them? Are they messages you would like to promote for others? Would you teach them to your children? Or other people's children? Would you teach them to yourself as a child? What do you think of these messages now?

_____
_____
_____
_____
_____

BODY ACCEPTANCE

THERE IS A REASON IT IS CALLED PROGRAMMING

Programming is the messages we have all received about body weight, shape, appearance, emotions (and how to manage them), and other important things. These messages can come from family, friends, media, or other sources. We cannot go back and rewrite our past. Our histories call for acceptance and not control. However, being *attached* to the programming we have accumulated through our lives can make our history stick with us in the present. For example, if you were teased for being "fat" or "ugly" as a child, you most likely are carrying around a bit of "programming" that is telling you that you are "fat" and "ugly" now. If you, like most women in this culture, saw images of thin or airbrushed models held up as an ideal of "beautiful" or "good," you are probably carrying programming that tells you that this is what "good" is. If you were told as a child not to cry, you may have programming that negative emotions are dangerous and to be avoided.

The fact that you are carrying these things around is not a problem. We are all "programmed." It is the fact that we tend to lose perspective and automatically *believe* and *behave* based on what our programming tells us, that leads us to lose sight of the fact that it is just "programming." We did not choose to be programmed with these messages, and just because we carry them around in our minds does not make them more "true," or the evaluations we base on them any more "right," than any other type of experience. Some programming messages may be useful to us now, and others may not. To find out, though, we have to identify what our programming *is*. Here is a place to start:

1. Think about a significant event from your childhood. Write it down here:

   _____

   _____

Can you identify some programming that you are carrying about this event? What did you conclude about the way the world worked? What did you conclude about yourself? Have you formulated other rules based on this experience? Write down as many of these as you can identify.

_____

_____

_____

_____

_____

2. Think of your favorite TV shows as a child, as an adolescent, and currently. Now see whether you can identify some programming that you are carrying from those programs. What did you conclude about the way the world worked? What did you conclude about yourself? Write down as many of these as you can identify.

_____

_____

_____

_____

3. Think of your favorite books and magazines as a child, as an adolescent, and currently. Can you identify any programming that you are carrying from this reading material? What did you conclude about the way the world worked? What did you conclude about yourself? Write down as many of these as you can identify.

4. Are there other sources of programming that affected you growing up? (Friends, school, toys?) List what you learned and what programming you think you carry from these as well.

The next two pages are blank, so you can draw or collage family, peer, or media messages you've received about your body. As you draw, write, or paste in messages, notice these messages as objects. They are not gospel truths given from a divine authority. They are pieces of paper; pencil or pen lines. Do you agree with them? Do you want to sell or give these ideas to others? Are they helpful ideas that have improved your life or brought you joy? Or have they treated you badly, these ideas? Consider these questions while you draw or collage in the programming you are carrying now.

BODY ACCEPTANCE

MY PROGRAMMING

MY PROGRAMMING

Orwell's Circus Dog

George Orwell, in a 1944 essay, said, "Circus dogs jump when the trainer cracks his whip, but the really well-trained dog is the one that turns his somersault when there is no whip" (Orwell, Orwell, & Angus, 1968). The metaphor of a whip is a good one: Many pieces of the most hurtful programming you carry may have come to you in the form of or alongside abuse: cruelty from peers, weight-based abuse from physicians or family members, neglect (e.g., food deprivation), or physical or sexual abuse. The "training" that results from these abusive experiences can be extremely powerful, and having experienced it, you too may be still turning somersaults the way an abuser trained you to even if the abuser is no longer present in your life, or even alive. Even if your programming didn't come from abuse, but simply from stewing in the cultural messages we all receive, it is worth considering if you see in your life any resemblance to Orwell's "well-trained dog." Are there messages you were given that hurt, but that you are still following? What does Orwell's quote mean to you?

_____

_____

_____

_____

Albert Ellis and *The Folklore of Sex*

The famous psychologist, cognitive therapist, and researcher Albert Ellis did a study of mass media output in 1950, called *The Folklore of Sex*, that shows how we circus dogs have been trained to jump for decades in the US, at least. He conducted an in-depth study of all mass-media products available to him on January 1 of that year, including all newspapers, plays, songs, radio, and television (Ellis, 1951). He found that for both men and women, *female physical beauty* was the most emphasized characteristic for a happy relationship. What do you make of this? Do you think things have changed? Why don't you find out? Take a look around the space where you are. Are there any magazines or books besides this one? Do you have a computer, iPad, or smartphone handy? Is the radio or a music player on? Take a look at your social media feeds, email, and any websites you regularly visit. Look up the lyrics of any songs that are currently playing. Look at the books or magazines. What messages can you find in the media available right now in your immediate environment about what will cause a happy romantic relationship for men? For women? Write about and document your findings here. Feel free to paste in pictures in the margins if you like.

_____

_____

_____

_____

_____

_____

_____

TURNING DOWN PROGRAMMING, TUNING IN TO YOUR BODY

You may be beginning to realize just how many messages you have unwittingly received about your body from sources you did not choose. You may wish that we could get rid of this programming, since it is so pervasive and harmful, or at least control it in our own minds. If so, I have some more bad news: *programming cannot be turned off!* It will *always* be available and chattering at us. However, programming can be *turned down*. Not turned down as in reducing the volume, but turned down as in refusal: we can *refuse* to use it as a guide to our life choices. How can we do that?

One way is by *tuning in* to it, becoming more aware of the programming, and aware that it is programming, and that we have a choice about how to respond to it. I have a suggestion for you about a difficult but important exercise in both tuning in and turning down media programming in particular.

A Different Kind of Diet

Here is the exercise: For one week, go on a media diet. Take a break from all sources of media. Turn off the television and the radio. Refrain from using the internet (apart from work research), listening to music, or playing games. Put away any magazines and books (apart from work reading). Replace this media time with movement and physical activities from your magic wand fantasy. Try to eliminate as much media as you can. People often find that this exercise sounds difficult – turning off all sources of media is very threatening, when most of us spend so much time connected to music, online media, and news. I can tell you that engaging with this exercise often has a powerful payoff, and, after all, it is only one week. Anyone can manage one week! I encourage you to commit to at least one aspect of this "media diet." You may commit to engage in this entire activity or only some portion of it (such as only avoiding Facebook, for example). When you do this activity, it is likely that negative emotions, as well as positive ones will arise. Notice what emerges as you take your break from media. There is space below to journal about your experiences with the media diet each day of the one-week break. There are questions each day to consider, but feel free to note whatever you observe.

Media Diet

Day 1: How are you feeling about the first day of your media diet? Is it difficult to give media up? Do you notice any cravings (already!) for your Instagram feed or to check email or listen to music? What else do you notice?

BODY ACCEPTANCE

Day 2: How is it to do without music? Without television? In the car, at your desk, at home? Is the silence difficult, or perhaps peaceful? Does loneliness emerge with the television turned off? Are there shows you are missing? What other aspects do you notice?

_____
_____
_____
_____
_____
_____

Day 3: Do you notice any shifts in what you are thinking or feeling? Do negative emotions arise? Which ones? How about any positive emotions? Welcome whatever emotions show up and be curious about them. What are they? What are they telling you?

_____
_____
_____
_____
_____
_____

Day 4: What about shifts in your behavior? How are you spending your time? Have you done any magic wand activities? How much space has shown up your day? Has it been difficult to fill? What else are you noticing?

_____
_____
_____
_____
_____
_____

Day 5: Have you "cheated" and looked at any media? What was that like? How did it feel? What did you notice? Or have you stuck with it faithfully? What other aspects are you noticing?

_____
_____

Day 6: You're almost finished with your media diet. What changes have occurred over the course of the week? Did you notice any shifts in your programming? Did it get louder, quieter, or stay the same? What other aspects are important to consider now?

Day 7: This is the last day of the media diet. What have been the lessons learned for you? Some people find that they want to continue (or continue in part) some aspect of the diet: Was this true for you? Were there any forms of media you felt like you wanted to give up permanently after the break, or cut down on consuming? What does it feel like to resume media consumption? What do you notice as your turn back on the television, the stereo, the computer, and pick up your books and papers?

Becoming aware of programming is a process, and is not completed overnight, or in a week. But noticing programming as programming is a first step in learning how to live according to your own values, dreams, and wishes. Not by the whip of Orwell's circus dog.

The media diet you just completed offered one way to become more aware of your programming, and more aware that it *is* programming, and that you have a choice in how you respond to it and whether you will follow its direction or turn it down. You might have noticed that your programming actually got louder and more insistent when you turned off your media for a week; if so, that's part of the process of awareness: You are tuning in to the programming and hearing it loud and clear. Tuning in is one of the first steps involved in turning it down. There are several other important ways to tune in to programming that we can try.

BODY ACCEPTANCE

What Does Your Body Really Look like?

Programmed ideas and beliefs about what women's bodies can and should look like can affect something as simple as our sense of self-awareness and body image. To observe this process at work with your own body self-awareness, try the *Silhouette Tracing Exercise*. To begin, find a roll of butcher paper or other large paper (or tape sheets of paper together). Roll out a long sheet or two – a little taller than you – and tape it to the wall so that it ends just a little over the top of your head. Use a marker to draw on the butcher paper your own silhouette. Don't use a shadow or other reference point, just draw your best guess at your body's size and shape from head to toe on the paper. Now take it down (being careful to keep the tape seams if you taped several sheets together) and lay it on the floor. Lie on top of it so that your head touches the top of your drawing. Now have a friend take a different-colored marker and trace carefully around your body to make a silhouette. (If you are a wheelchair user, you may want to draw images both in and outside of your chair. You may also want to have a friend help transfer you to the floor to trace a "standing" image, as well as have a friend use an overhead projector to cast an image of you on the wall and trace an image of you in your wheelchair.) Once the images are complete, compare them. Are they the same? Similar? How different are they? Most people's silhouettes are not exactly accurate, or even particularly close. Is this true for you? Are there places on your body where you were more or less accurate? Perhaps your belly is wider than you thought, or your hips. Perhaps your head is larger or smaller than you imagined. Perhaps you are shorter than you thought, or taller. Here is a bit of space to both journal about and draw in what you noticed during this exercise:

Silhouette Tracing: What Did I Observe?

_____

_____

_____

_____

_____

_____

Many people overestimate their actual size, and others underestimate. It is neither possible nor necessary to have an "accurate" sense of self. Our bodies are always changing, for one thing, as is our awareness of them as we move through the world. Our programming, the thoughts and feelings and messages and rules we picked up about our bodies along the way, also ebbs and flows, with different "channels" of programming coming into our awareness and shaping our body images at different times.

It is not actually important for you to have an accurate body image, nor is it important or meaningful to know in what way you were inaccurate in your body image. Body image and self-awareness fluctuates: if you repeated the exercise, you might notice a variety of changes. It is simply worth observing that our body images are often inaccurate, and that the image we hold of ourselves in our head is a product not only of feedback from our actual lived experiences inside our bodies, but also from a variety of rules and ideas we have learned about what bodies do and should look like.

Another way of beginning to observe your own body in a non-judgmental way is an exercise called the *mindful mirror,* and it may help you to begin to observe your programming about your own body without buying into it. To do this exercise, you'll need a full-length mirror in a private place. You can do this exercise nude, or if you prefer, in a swimsuit or underwear. Before beginning this exercise, I encourage you to think about how artists think about and paint from live models. When drawing or painting from life, an artist can use any model – all genders, body sizes, shapes, and ages are potentially interesting subjects to paint. And whatever the artist thinks of the model's appearance, any judgments the artist might have are not necessarily helpful to him or her in translating the model's image to the canvas or page. Instead, the artist looks carefully at the model, but is thinking of the model's body in terms of color, light, shape: a line of gray down the back of the arm where the shadow hits it, the rich mahogany triangle of skin between the eyebrows before the lighter rectangle of brown down the ridge of the nose. As you complete this exercise, you will be describing your body to yourself as an artist might.

Another way of imagining the eyes you will be trying to put on and look through as you do this exercise is to imagine a space alien trying to describe your body, the first body this alien person has encountered on Earth. The alien has never seen a body, and does not even have a concept of "eyes" or "toes," much less "pretty" or "ugly," to help organize what the alien is seeing. The alien will describe what is seen in terms of shape, color, and from a stance of curiosity, since presumably the alien will be reporting back about the strange creatures of Earth! If it does not seem familiar to look at yourself through artist's eyes, try looking at yourself through the space alien's eyes.

To do the exercise, stand naked or in your underwear or swimwear in front of the mirror. Begin at the very top of your head and work your way downwards to your toes. Look carefully and mindfully, and out loud, observe everything that you see using the eyes of the space alien or the artist. Describe colors, shapes, textures. Avoid using body part names as short hand if you can. For example, instead of saying "My eyebrows are brown and close together. I have wrinkles between my eyebrows," you might say, "There is a strip of dark brown short hair in the upper middle left side of the creamy peach-colored egg-shape, and another similar strip on the right side. Both strips are about a ¼ inch wide, and they have an arch shape. Some of the hairs lie parallel to one another, and others are set to one side or in a different direction. The two strips are about ¾ of an inch apart, and there are three small parallel lines in the skin between them, which are a light gray color."

As you do this exercise, your mind will provide a variety of thoughts and feelings, including judgments. That's fine. Just notice them as you go, by saying them out loud and labeling them as thoughts, feelings, judgments, etc.: "Oh, now I notice that I'm having the thought that I look old with all these wrinkles on my face." "Now I notice that I'm feeling sad." "Now I notice that I'm feeling cold, and there are small brown bumps that have shown up along my arms, each with a hair in the center." Notice these thoughts or experiences, then return to describing with the artist's or alien's eyes. Whatever thoughts, feelings, and sensations emerge while you do this exercise, you can notice them and describe them out loud. Spend at least 20 minutes on this exercise. Really take your time and go slowly, describing each part of you with the artist's or alien's eyes. What do you notice?

BODY ACCEPTANCE

The Mindful Mirror: My Observations

_____
_____
_____
_____
_____
_____
_____
_____

Mindful Movement

Another area to explore mindfully is movement. If you have struggled with body image or weight concerns, you may have a complicated relationship with "exercise." Simply living in a thin-ideal, weight-stigmatizing culture provides us all with lots of judgmental negative programming related to moving our bodies: "No pain, no gain!" And yet movement is a major way your body has the opportunity to experience the world. We will work in future chapters with movement, but, for now, you might try doing any kind of movement you like with your full, mindful attention. You can choose a simple, daily movement done very briefly, such as a walk around the block or a stretch in your bed or chair before rising. Or you can choose a more complex, challenging, or unfamiliar movement to experiment with, perhaps rock-climbing, or swimming, or dance, or a brief, hard run. Any kind of movement can be experienced mindfully. In any kind of mindfulness, including when doing mindful movement, you simply notice what arises, including thoughts, emotions, and physical sensations. Vary the speed or intensity of your movement and notice what shifts with your mind, emotions, and physical sensations. Notice how your body feels before the movement, and afterwards. What do you observe?

_____
_____
_____
_____
_____
_____

Now that you have completed these exercises in observing your body, your movements, and your thoughts and judgments related to body image, you have already begun learning two essential self-acceptance skills: Mindfulness and non-judgment. These skills will be valuable to you in helping to tune in to your programming, which, in turn, will help you turn it down when you don't want to be guided by it. You may wish to explore these skills in detail with the help of a therapist, or by formal meditation practice on your own, using guided meditations. The Free Mindfulness Project (www.freemindfulness.org) website, for example, has a variety of downloadable mindfulness meditation recordings. Marsha

Linehan (1993) has written about non-judgment as a skill. The therapist companion volume to this book also has detailed information about these skills which you can read and discuss with your therapist.

IS THERE A BOMB IN YOUR MIND?

One reason to experiment with mindfulness is to become more aware of what is happening inside our minds. Have you ever had painful thoughts about yourself or your body that caused depression or unhappiness, thoughts that you wanted to avoid? You may have felt that these thoughts were actually dangerous, as if thinking them might harm you in some way, as if these thoughts were actually bombs that might explode and ruin everything! Are these "dangerous thoughts" actually bombs?

Well, if they were bombs, they could harm you, or even kill you. Can your most dangerous, upsetting thoughts hurt you? I'd like you to take a moment and imagine in your mind, as vividly as you can, a bomb. Try describing the bomb here, and in the margin also draw a picture of it.

Envisioning a Bomb

_____

_____

_____

_____

_____

_____

_____

Do you have a clear picture of your bomb now? Can you make it any more vivid and clear? (If you can, go back and add some details to your drawing or your description.) Now that you have a vivid image, do you feel afraid? (Why or why not?) Are you willing to sit in the room with this imaginary bomb you have made? How long would you be willing to sit in the room with it? Can this bomb hurt you?

No. It's harmless. Let's see if we can make the thought more dangerous. Can you imagine actually building a bomb? Can you imagine developing the expertise to do that, constructing your bomb, placing it somewhere where it would go off and hurt or kill someone you dislike? What emotions emerge as you consider this more graphic and alarming set of thoughts? Perhaps you feel uncomfortable: "I'm not a violent person. Where is this author going with this? I would never do anything like this!" Perhaps you feel a rush of enjoyment; maybe there's someone in your life you enjoy imagining a vengeful fantasy about. And then perhaps you feel guilty, and embarrassed, or even ashamed or alarmed.

But whatever has shown up, notice this: Your thoughts are harmless. An imaginary bomb – no matter how vividly imagined – cannot harm anyone. Even detailed bomb-making instructions are harmless unless someone follows them and builds a bomb using behavior, not just in mind. While a real bomb can kill you, an imaginary one cannot – no matter how vividly you've imagined it!

You may have never thought about building a bomb until this moment, but ask yourself: Do you have thoughts that you feel are dangerous and harmful to have in your head? Perhaps you have thoughts that feel hurtful when you think them, that you would like out of your head. "I'm disgusting," might be one such thought. Or "life is hopeless." Do you think thoughts like these? Notice that these painful thoughts are also imaginary bombs. Even the worst thoughts we may have are not actual objects of mass destruction sitting in the room – they are just sounds in our heads. Nevertheless, we treat words and images as if they were very powerful and dangerous.

The point is, words – even words that feel very powerful, like "You're a disgusting, terrible person," or "If I do that, something terrible might happen" – are just sounds, just chatter, just something our minds do. Our minds cannot help it, and sometimes words are very important and helpful. But a thought you think is just a thought: Like the bomb-making instructions we envisioned a moment ago, even the worst or most painful thought is not necessarily anything you have to respond to. Still, minds are busy producing all these thoughts, and trying to convince us that they are important, and literally true. Sometimes we take our minds so literally that we do not even notice how busy they are chattering at us. We do not even see what they are doing.

Mindfulness is one way to watch all this chatter and the image of bomb provides another way: Perhaps we can think of these painful, "dangerous" thoughts as *defused* bombs. A defused bomb is a harmless hunk of metal! It may still look like a bomb, and have the shape of a bomb, but it is harmless. Would you be willing to sit in the room with a defused bomb? (If not, why not?) Thoughts, too, after we defuse them (or rather, notice that they are *already* defused, since, as you have seen, your thoughts never were actually dangerous), are still there. You still think them, but you're able to notice that they are not harmful, that you need not do anything about them.

REFERENCES

Ellis, A. (1951). *The folklore of sex* (1st ed.). New York: C. Boni.

Linehan, M. (1993). *Cognitive-behavioral treatment of borderline personality disorder*. New York: Guilford.

Orwell, G., Orwell, S. (Ed.), & Angus, I. (Ed.). (1968). *The collected essays, journalism and letters of George Orwell: Vol 03, As I Please, 1943–1945*. London: Secker and Warburg.

5
From Mindfulness to Self-Acceptance

At this point in your journey, you have completed all the foundational work you will need to help you become ready for the difficult task of self-acceptance. You have examined how controlling your weight and negative body image has worked in your life. You have learned about the programming we all carry that led you down this path in the first place, and you have learned some tools to hold that programming more lightly, especially mindfulness and bomb defusion. If you have a regular mindfulness practice of some kind, whether formal meditation or mindful movement or observation done regularly, you are ready to engage in self-acceptance.

Noticing thoughts as thoughts and practicing mindfulness, in general, is *already* one form of acceptance – that is, during mindfulness, we just *accept* whatever shows up in our minds and bodies. During a ten-minute mindfulness meditation, we try to observe what shows up, but not change it. We just accept it as it is. However, this is not our usual approach to emotional pain.

We often try to control negative emotions and feelings about our bodies by avoiding or trying to control situations that we think will bring them up. This is avoidance. Self-acceptance is an alternative. Acceptance is not the same as liking or loving a situation. It doesn't take away pain; it simply allows you to sit compassionately with your pain. "Loving" or liking your body or your moods is not a requirement for self-acceptance. Self-acceptance is something you *do*, not something you feel.

BUILDING ACCEPTANCE BY EXPERIENCING

How do we practice acceptance of a difficult thought or emotion? It's not easy, but it is simple: To practice acceptance, you just *deliberately experience* whatever has been previously avoided. If previously you "pulled away," now you will "lean in." While trying these self-acceptance exercises, you are invited to mindfully observe whatever emerges.

It is important to keep a daily mindfulness practice of some kind, such as mindfulness meditation, as you enter this part of the program. Mindfulness skills, as they develop, will be helpful in your acceptance practice, in remaining mindful in distressing situations. The next step in this program will be to use these mindfulness skills to approach situations that you previously avoided. These exercises may be the most difficult exercises in the book. They are also the most exciting, and important, so be sure not to skip them.

Self-acceptance involves willingly experiencing painful, difficult, or avoided situations. You may wonder: Why would I do that? I already have plenty of pain in my life! I'm trying to avoid pain, not experience more!

Self-acceptance practice is different from the pain you are already experiencing and struggling to escape on a daily basis, because it is a deliberate, mindful, and intentional experience. All of us have experienced emotional pain. But have you ever *deliberately entered* a situation that you knew would being up emotional pain, just to experience it fully? For most people, that is a new experience, and it is a new experience I encourage you to experiment with. After all, this is your book and your work: It's all up to you, and no one will know if you don't try an exercise out. You are free to choose. Would you like to try a self-acceptance experiment now?

BODY ACCEPTANCE

Amy's Painful Situations

Difficulty Level	Situation	Type (Food-Related, Guilt/Shame Food, Body Image, Bad Moods)
1	Walking through the halls at work	Body image
2	Ice cream	Guilt/shame food
3	Cookies	Guilt/shame food
4	Not liking what I've been served	Food-related
5	Going to a restaurant I've never been to and not knowing what the seating is like	Body image
6	Eating alone at home or driving	Food-related
7	Buffet-style parties	Food-related
8	Feeling like I have no friends	Bad moods
9	Fast food	Guilt/shame food
10	Going out alone	Bad moods
11	Eating in front of my mom	Food-related
12	Not having access to food at night	Food-related
13	My mom being unsympathetic or unkind	Bad moods
14	Not fitting comfortably in chairs	Body image
15	Guilt around my extramarital affair	Bad moods
16	Trying on or shopping for clothes	Body image
17	Someone coming to visit my messy apartment	Bad moods
18	Posting a picture on a dating site	Body image
19	Having someone from work see me binging at the Chinese buffet	Food-related
20	Going to the beach wearing a fatkini	Body image

Let's begin by choosing the right self-acceptance experiment for you, both for now and more for later use. You will be practicing with situations revolving around food, situations revolving around body image, and situations revolving around negative moods and emotions. Amy, a 26-year-old nurse, created her list of painful situations, which you can see above. Her list is in order of difficulty, and she has noted in the margin what type of situation each is.

Amy's Painful Situations
Like Amy, you, too, are asked to make a list of situations that distress you, related to body image, food, and just unpleasant emotional situations in general. (See table on page 51.) You should choose situations that you often or always seek to avoid, but that you have the opportunity to practice regularly. For example, initially, Amy chose "my mom dying," as a situation that would be difficult for her and cause bad moods. Hopefully, her mom dying will not happen soon or regularly! Thus it is not a good situation for practice. Choose situations that either come up regularly or you could voluntarily arrange in some way. Amy's list is organized from least to most difficult. When you make your list, don't try to organize it that way at first. Just list difficult situations. Try to make sure you have at least three situations from each category (body-image related, food-related, guilt- or shame-inducing foods you try to avoid eating, and situations that bring up bad moods). Also, try to change emotions to situations. For example, Amy listed "guilt about my extramarital affair," a feeling, on her list, as something she found difficult and tried to avoid. When her therapist asked her "What situations make you feel guilty about

My Painful Situations

Difficulty Level	Situation	Type (Food-Related, Guilt/Shame Food, Body Image, Bad Moods)	✓ When Experienced

the affair? If you *wanted* to feel extra guilty about the affair, what would you do?" Amy said, "I'd talk with his wife, who is a co-worker of mine at work, about work-related things. Whenever I talk to her, I always feel super guilty, so I try to stay out of her way, even though I sometimes need to work with her on projects." For your list, if there are feelings or thoughts you are avoiding, try to figure out and write down what situations reliably bring up those unpleasant feelings and thoughts.

When you have a list of 15–20 painful situations, you can use the left-hand column of the blank table to put them in order. Use the number 1 to designate the easiest situation on the list. This should be a situation that, while unpleasant, you can tolerate, and maybe have to regularly experience. Then, use bigger numbers for more painful situations, up to 15 or 20, which may be situations you can't imagine experiencing willingly ever, at all. Don't worry about that for now: It's your list, and you don't have to do anything you don't want to do! Just make the list and put it in order of difficulty.

My Painful Situations

With this list in hand, you are ready to approach the first (easiest) situation on your list. You will experience each situation on your list, one at a time, easiest situations first. In completing these difficult self-acceptance exercises, it is useful to imagine yourself climbing a mountain. When you approach each situation (especially the more difficult situations), you will feel as if you are scaling a very difficult mountain, which requires all of your fortitude and resolve. Just looking at it might make you feel scared and dizzy! As you begin to climb the mountain, it will become more difficult.

For example, for Amy, walking through the halls at work in her fat body made her feel very anxious, especially if she went by her co-workers' cubicles and people socialized with her and could see her. She avoided walking the halls at work, even to the point of attending meetings remotely, by phone from her desk, to avoid walking down the hall. When she planned to walk around her office, going by each cubicle, she felt fearful, and had the urge to wear a poncho or shawl so that she could better hide her stomach from her co-workers' eyes. However, for acceptance practice, since she was trying to lean in and experience her fears, she did not do this, but simply went around the office in her regular work clothes. As she began to walk around the office, she felt even more scared and ashamed. She was beginning to climb her mountain, and the climb was getting steeper and more difficult. She had the urge to go back to her office. She reached the peak of the mountain, and her peak level of distress, when a co-worker she felt judged her weight came out from a cubicle and complimented her on her outfit, noting that she hadn't seen Amy around in a while, and that it was good to see her. Amy had the urge to run and hide, but made conversation with her co-worker. To her surprise, after her co-worker returned to her cubicle, Amy felt less scared and ashamed, and could comfortably complete her planned circuit of the cubicles in her building. She was on the downward slope of the mountain, and things were a little easier now. By the time she returned to her own office, she did not feel any shame or fear at all, which surprised her. Furthermore, she told her therapist that she now felt she could maybe go to the next scheduled meeting at her office, rather than calling in to it.

This is how acceptance often works, although I encourage you to observe whether this is true for you, rather than believing what you read. But see if this is true for your self-acceptance practice: Your negative emotions begin to build as you lead up to practicing, and they will increase in intensity as you begin the practice. You will have the urge to stop the practice, but I discourage this, because going back down the mountain the way you came, although it will usually temporarily alleviate your distress, makes the mountain taller and more difficult next time you try to climb it. (If you do end an acceptance activity prematurely, see if this is true for you by trying the same activity again in a few days. Is it more difficult after you avoided it?) Instead of going down the mountain, continue to climb toward your distress. You will reach a peak of distress at some point. Remain in the situation when this occurs, even if you want to run and hide. Do you notice your distress dropping as you summit the mountain and begin to go down the other side? When do the bad feelings ebb away entirely? Does it seem easier to approach that situation again? Try the first situation on your list, and make some notes here about your experiences climbing the acceptance mountain.

The Acceptance Mountain

_____
_____
_____
_____
_____
_____
_____

Avoidance in the Midst of Acceptance

One problem that may come up during your acceptance practice is avoidance in the midst of acceptance. If you avoid in the midst of acceptance, it will prevent you from summiting the acceptance mountain and experiencing the drop in distress on the other side. But what does "avoidance in the midst of acceptance" mean, and how do you avoid it?

To illustrate avoidance in the midst of acceptance, imagine a rollercoaster. If you enjoy rollercoasters, then you are probably enjoying this mental image, too: thinking about your last trip to Six Flags, or your next one! But if you don't like rollercoasters, you're probably thinking thoughts of non-acceptance: "No way! Not me on the rollercoaster! I can't do that." But let's say you want to go on a rollercoaster, for some reason, even though you are terrified of the fast cars and the upside down drops. Maybe you are trying to impress a friend, or a date, or maybe someone dared you to do it and said they'd give you $20 if you would go. Maybe you're going with a child you love, who isn't tall enough to go unless you go. If you hate riding on rollercoasters, what do you do to try to avoid the experience of riding on a rollercoaster, even while you're riding the rollercoaster? Maybe you close your eyes, or hang on extra tight, or make the attendant triple check that your seat is closed and locked! All these things are avoidance in the midst of acceptance. And what do they do? They teach you that rollercoasters are to be feared and avoided! When you are doing acceptance practice, watch out for suggestions your mind makes about how to avoid in the midst of acceptance, and don't avoid. The goal is to feel the feelings you are trying to avoid. So if rollercoaster riding is on your list: Open your eyes! Don't check the seat! Don't hang on tight! Just sit back and experience the ride.

Some people wonder why they should deliberately experience things they have avoided. I really encourage you to find this out for yourself: just try experimenting with what you notice and what occurs when you do engage in this strange and counterintuitive experience of doing things you have avoided and feeling things you have avoided. To do these exercises is very challenging, but it also has an important payoff in experience.

Before going on, take your time and begin to experience the situations on your list, one at a time. This week, which acceptance exercises will you try? (Start with the lowest numbers – the easiest items – on your list. Your mind will give you lots of reasons why it is not practical or possible or advisable to do this now, and will suggest all sorts of workarounds, like skipping this part and going on. Thank your mind for all these thoughts, and go ahead and commit to doing the first acceptance exercises now anyway.) Remember to avoid avoidance in the midst of acceptance. Mindfully observe the mountain as you climb. Check the acceptance practices off your list as you complete them. Note which ones you are going to do this week here, and write out how and when you'll do them:

BODY ACCEPTANCE

Acceptance Practice #1

What I'll Do And How: _____

_____

_____

_____

_____

_____

When: _____

As you work through the remainder of this book, in each chapter you'll be prompted to write out what acceptance exercises you want to work on during this time, and given space to reflect on what you experienced with the acceptance exercises you have already tried. This is the most challenging, and the most rewarding, aspect of your recovery in this book, so I wish you well, and am cheering for you as you begin your practice.

6
Producing Your Own Programming

Before we discuss the topic of this chapter, how did your first acceptance practices go? What did you do? What did you experience? Did you notice increasing negative emotions as you went up the mountain, and decreasing emotions as you remained in the situation? (Did you bail out halfway or three-quarters of the way up the mountain and not fully experience acceptance? Did you avoid in the midst of acceptance? What did you notice if that happened?) Did you notice any differences between what your mind expected or predicted out of the experience and what actually occurred? Journal about your experiences here:

_____
_____
_____
_____
_____
_____
_____
_____
_____
_____

What will you do for your next acceptance practices? (If you bailed out of your mountain climb, or if you avoided in the midst of acceptance, you will want to do the same acceptance practice again, working on staying present and not avoiding. If this was you, you may find the second practice more challenging than the first. Have compassion for yourself as you do this difficult exercise a second time, and stay with it.) If your first experience was completed without escaping or avoiding the situation, you are ready to go on to the next situations on your list, regardless of what emotions showed up for you during your first practice. Congratulations on attempting and completing your first acceptance practice! Now, what's next? (Notice if your mind chatters reasons you can't do this next practice, and thank it for those thoughts as you make your plans.)

ACCEPTANCE PRACTICE #2

What I'll Do And How: _____
_____
_____

BODY ACCEPTANCE

_____
_____
_____

When:_____

DIFFICULTIES WITH SELF-ACCEPTANCE: SIZE DISCRIMINATION

One problem you may face in practicing your avoided activities is size discrimination. Evidence of discrimination against fat people, in general, and fat women, in particular, is sobering. Fat people are stereotyped as emotionally impaired, socially handicapped, and as possessing negative personality traits. They are denigrated by doctors, nurses, peers, small children, and even their own parents. (See Puhl & Heuer, 2009, for a review.)

Health professionals discriminate against fat patients in ways that harm their health across the lifespan. Many fat patients report being evaluated only for their weight – when they go in for an ear infection or birth control they may get a lecture about obesity. Even doctors who do not mention fat may be discriminating against fat patients. Using a standard size (rather than a large size) blood pressure cuff on fat patients can give a blood pressure reading that is inaccurately high, by between 8 and 12 mm of mercury – enough of a difference to be largely responsible for the research finding that fat people are at greater risk for hypertension (Palatini & Parati, 2011).

Fat people are discriminated against at work, school, and in other domains. Roehling (1999), in a review of the literature, concluded that the evidence of consistent, significant discrimination against fat employees is overwhelming, and that evidence of discrimination was found at every stage of the employment cycle, from selection and placement, to compensation, promotion, and discharge.

Fatness is also unique as a focus of discrimination in that people who experience it are given the task of avoiding it by changing their bodies. This is not really possible for most people over the long term, and it is not something we suggest for other victims of discrimination. Women are not asked to become male and avoid gender discrimination, for example. The most appropriate response to any kind of discrimination is to help society become more enlightened, and to stand up to discrimination so no one has to experience unfair bias.

What have been your experiences with discrimination (size discrimination and/or other kinds of discrimination? How have you handled this problem? What strategies have worked for you in terms of coping with discrimination or standing up against it?

_____
_____
_____
_____
_____
_____
_____
_____

Discrimination of any kind is wrong. _You deserve better._

Dealing with Size Discrimination at the Doctor's Office

One of the most dangerous and stressful places you may experience size discrimination (as well as other forms of discrimination) is at the doctor's office. *You deserve unbiased, compassionate medical care* no matter what kind of body you have. If you are not getting it, even if you have never received such care, you deserve it. You are entitled to demand it. Also, you are entitled to push back against biased care. You are entitled to refuse to be routinely weighed, if you wish, to write complaint letters, to speak to patient advocates. Shaming you for your weight or insisting you lose weight before receiving a medical procedure or intervention isn't evidence-based or ethical. If this is happening to you, I want to reassure you that it is wrong. Nevertheless, most of my patients report being treated this way some of the time, and most have avoided medical care they needed and put their health at risk because of this shaming, discriminatory treatment. How can you take care of yourself when size (and other) discrimination by doctors is so common and toxic?

You can search the HAES Community or Association for Size Diversity and Health websites (which you will find below in the resources section) to find doctors or other health professionals who explicitly practice HAES (Health At Every Size). If you cannot find a non-stigmatizing health provider in your community, a back-up option is to advocate for yourself with the providers you have to deal with. *You should not have to do this.* However, educating biased and discriminatory doctors may help you get better care, and it may help other people in the future. Blogger Ragen Chastain has a downloadable, free set of "How to Talk To Your Doctor" cards that you can print off, laminate, and bring to your doctor's office. (These are available here: https://danceswithfat.wordpress.com/2013/04/01/what-to-say-at-the-doctors-office) Having a card handy can help you communicate when discriminatory behavior leaves you feeling stressed, vulnerable, or tearful. Similarly, Linda Bacon has a message for healthcare providers you can give your doctor, available here: https://lindabacon.org/HAESbook/pdf_files/HAES_Providing%20Sensitive%20Care.pdf. Doing these things for yourself offers an opportunity to practice acceptance of many painful emotions, even though the discrimination which is prompting the emotion is unacceptable and wrong. It also is an opportunity to practice one of the skills of this chapter, which involves responding creatively to your own programming.

PRODUCING YOUR OWN PROGRAMMING

One way of turning down (refusing) programming that you didn't choose – as well as responding more effectively to size discrimination by doctors or anyone else – is by producing your own programming, so it reflects your creativity, self-expression, and values. If you have begun your practice of accepting and experiencing your difficult situations, you may have already noticed that your programming shows up whenever you try to do something difficult, or something your programming says you can't or shouldn't do. And you may have already noticed that when you disobey the programming and do an acceptance practice anyway, the experience is nothing like what your mind says it will be. Nevertheless, the mind continues to chatter programming at you! Programming can't be unlearned, and, luckily, that's not our goal. The goal of this chapter is to help you find your own unique voice to add to our cultural messages about weight and shape, to help you produce programming, not just consume what is programmed into you at random.

We did not choose most of the programming in our minds. It is just there, floating around. It is in some ways similar to a television or cable box, in that there are multiple channels of programming available to us (in our minds) at any time. Unlike a television, however, our minds cannot be turned off. We can sometimes change the channel, and choose to attend to various different "stations" in our mental programming, but we do not have total control over what passes over the screen, although we can notice it and comment on it. We can also make our own programming, create our own messages and share them with others, especially if we don't like anything that is "on" in our minds. As programmers, we may not have much influence or power or budget to promote our ideas. But a good idea, a helpful and creative piece of programming, as you know, can go viral even without its creator being so powerful, and have a much bigger influence that you might imagine.

One way to begin producing your own programming is to stop whatever you are currently doing to distribute the arbitrary, unhelpful programming you have already learned. Notice that this does not mean you stop having or hearing your own programming: Your mind may continue to chatter highly negative and judgmental body and diet talk no matter what your mouth does. And thank your mind for those chattery thoughts! They are fine, they are welcome, and they are helpful in learning the process of being mindfully aware of them and choosing how to respond to them. So let me be very clear: What we are about to do is not about changing your mind. It is about changing your mouth and your behavior to reflect your values and your self-acceptance practice.

One way to begin is by creating what therapist Deb Burgard calls a "body disparagement-free zone." This is a physical space where you commit to not disparaging your own or others' bodies. Note that it is not a *mental* space. Your mind may continue its judgmental chatter, and that's totally fine and to be expected and mindfully observed. This is a *physical* space where you agree not to make negatively judgmental comments about your own or others' bodies. Perhaps it is at home, or in your office, or in your kitchen, or at your gym. Dr. Burgard has doorhangers you can obtain to hang up and remind yourself of the physical space you are creating. You can see them at her website here, and order them; the first one is free: www.bodypositive.com/doorhangers.htm. Or, you can design your own doorhanger or sign to put up. Where will you put your body disparagement-free zone? Write it here.

_____

Another way to produce your own programming is simply to begin talking about your self-acceptance journey in public, whether with friends and family, on social media, or in more public forums. Perhaps you are curious about being more public with your self-acceptance, but fearful or uncertain about sharing your experiences with others. Or perhaps you are ready to explore being a self-acceptance role model for others. Perhaps you are not certain what you think about self-acceptance at this point, especially if (and this is likely) you do not feel any self-acceptance for your own body inside. That feeling – if you have it – is fine, and welcome. You do not need to learn to "love" your body, or feel "accepting" of it, in the Accept Yourself! process. Self-acceptance is not a feeling; it's a series of behaviors designed to help you achieve your dreams and goals. (Remember your magic wand fantasy?) One behavior to explore is reading about and interacting with others who are engaging in self and size-acceptance.

Resources for Programming the No-Self-Judgment Channel

How do you program your own "no-self-judgment channel" in your mind or in the world? What resources are there to explore in learning about self-acceptance? Besides hanging a doorhanger, how can you send the message to others that self-acceptance is being practiced here in your life, and is perhaps an option for others to practice as well?

There are many ways of both obtaining and sending a message that self-acceptance is possible and discrimination based on size is unacceptable. Here's a short list of resources that might offer a place to begin:

Books
- *Health At Every Size*, by Linda Bacon. A classic introduction to the HAES concept.
- *Get Out Of Your Mind And Into Your Life*, by Steven Hayes. An Acceptance and Commitment Therapy (ACT) workbook designed to help experience and accept different emotions, while living a valued life.
- *The Unapologetic Fat Girl's Guide To Exercise And Other Incendiary Acts*, by Hanne Blank. A funny, breezy manual to help fat women explore physical exercise and movement without a weight loss agenda.
- *Yoga XXL*, by Ingrid Kollak. A yoga sourcebook with lots of illustrations of fat women.
- *Eat, Drink, And Be Mindful*, by Susan Albers. An introduction to mindful eating.

- *Body Respect*, by Linda Bacon and Lucy Aphramor, debunks weight loss myths and addresses the role of weight stigma and discrimination in health.
- *The Obesity Myth*, by Paul Campos. A detailed, although now somewhat dated, look at the science behind weight and shape.
- *The Diet Survivor's Handbook*, by Judith Matz and Ellen Frankel. A workbook to help develop a healthy relationship with food for chronic dieters.
- *Eat What You Love, Love What You Eat*, by Michelle May. A mindful eating self-help program to address binge-eating difficulties.
- *Fat Politics*, by J. Eric Oliver. Discusses the political aspects of obesity science and science reporting, as well as reviewing the evidence about weight, shape, and health.
- *What's Wrong with Fat?*, by Abigail Saguy. Explores the concept of fatness and how this is defined from a sociological perspective.
- *Intuitive Eating*, by Evelyn Tribole and Elyse Resch. Focuses on learning to honor your own internal cues of appetite, hunger, and fullness.
- *Fat!So?*, by Marilyn Wann. Laugh-out-loud funny, creative guidebook to fat acceptance.
- *Living With Your Body And Other Things You Hate*, by Emily Sandoz and Troy DuFrene. An ACT guide to body image acceptance.
- *Lessons From The Fat-O-Sphere*, by Kate Harding and Marianne Kirby. Essays from the first fat acceptance bloggers, including the *Fantasy of Being Thin* and *Bachelorettes and Bathing Suits* essays discussed in this book.
- *Women En Large*, by Debbie Notkin and Laurie Toby Edison. A classic, gorgeous book of black-and-white photographs of nude, fat women, with their essays and commentary.
- *Things No One Will Tell Fat Girls*, by Jes Baker. Witty, amusing guidebook to body self-acceptance.
- *Big, Big Love*, by Hanne Blank. A sex and relationships manual for fat people and their lovers.

Websites
- Body Impolitic, http://laurietobyedison.com/body-impolitic-blog. Laurie Toby Edison's blog about photography and body image.
- The Fat Nutritionist, www.fatnutritionist.com. Covers nutrition issues from a HAES perspective.
- Dances with Fat, http://danceswithfat.wordpress.com. Dancer Ragen Chastain's blog covers dance and a variety of fat acceptance topics.
- IronFat, https://ironfatblog.wordpress.com. A second blog from Ragen Chastain, chronicling her journey to complete an Ironman Triathlon.
- The Militant Baker, www.themilitantbaker.com. Jes Baker's fashion, fat acceptance, and body image blog.
- The Association for Contextual Behavioral Science, www.contextualscience.org. Professional website for ACT.
- Body Positive, www.bodypositive.com. Deb Burgard's website, with extensive resources for body-image acceptance at all sizes.
- The Association for Size Diversity and Health, www.sizediversityandhealth.org. Professional organization for HAES practitioners.
- HAES Community, www.haescommunity.org. Allows you to sign a HAES pledge and find providers who have signed.
- The Problem with Poodle Science, www.youtube.com/watch?v=H89QQfXtc-k. A brief YouTube video addressing bias in the science of weight and health.
- The HAES Curriculum, http://haescurriculum.com. Three 30-minute PowerPoints with voiceover outlining the HAES principles.
- The Full Belly, https://thefullybelly.wordpress.com. My blog covering body acceptance for beginners.

How Will You Create a Self-Judgment-Free Channel and a Body Disparagement-Free Zone?

In what ways can you begin to create a self-judgment-free zone around yourself? In what ways can you send the message to other people that self-and body judgment is not acceptable?

_____
_____
_____

Are there books or websites you want to explore? Note them here, and take some time to journal your reactions. How can you use the information you've found here to help yourself?

_____
_____
_____
_____
_____

What is one action you can commit to take to create a self-judgment-free channel or a body disparagement-free zone? Write down one thing you will commit to here this week, including what you will do, how, and exactly when:

_____
_____
_____
_____
_____

REFERENCES

Palatini, P., & Parati, G. (2011). Blood pressure measurement in very obese patients: A challenging problem. *Journal of Hypertension, 29*(3), 425–429.

Puhl, R. M., & Heuer, C. A. (2009). The stigma of obesity: A review and update. *Obesity, 17*(5), 941–964.

Roehling, M. V. (1999). Weight-based discrimination in employment: Psychological and legal aspects. *Personnel Psychology, 52*(4), 969–1016.

PART 3
Can You Live the Life You've Always Wanted, in the Body You Have Now?

A Buddhist teaching holds "Your body is precious. It is our vehicle for awakening" (Kornfield, 1994). Without our minds and bodies – no matter how flawed – we are powerless. Our minds and bodies, whatever their vulnerabilities, however we feel about them, are our vehicles towards a valued, rich life. We have already discussed, in previous chapters, a new approach to taking care of your vehicle: Self-acceptance. The goal of this part of the book is to help you drive toward the kind of life you want, in terms of food, mental and physical health, and all the other things that really matter to you.

7
The Value of Feeding Yourself

Once again, before we discuss the topic of this chapter, how did your acceptance practices go this week? What did you do? What did you experience? Journal about your experiences here:

_____
_____
_____
_____
_____
_____
_____
_____
_____
_____

What will you do for your next acceptance practices? What is next on your list of painful situations? (Or would it be better to do your last acceptance exercise again, leaning in harder, before moving on?) Congratulations on continuing your acceptance practice! Now, what's next?

ACCEPTANCE PRACTICE #3

What I'll Do And How: _____

_____
_____
_____
_____
_____

When:_____

Acceptance practice will support you as you begin the process of driving where you really want to go. One place where you may have never considered where you really want to go is with food and eating. Are there food-related aspects to your magic wand fantasy? Many people, assured by the magic wand that they will have the body they want regardless of what they eat, imagine that they would eat indulgent treats. Perhaps you would eat platefuls of chocolate chip cookies, or all the ice cream you liked, or order pizza every Friday and eat half the pie, if you had the body you always wanted and didn't have to do anything to maintain it. Others imagine being freed from having to think about or worry about food at all, or from worry that others would judge their eating choices, or comment on them. Many other people simply don't mention food at all when they consider what they want if they could have the body they wished for, permanently.

And yet, lacking a magic wand, many people struggle with eating and food. The idea that gluttony causes an ugly, undesirable body is a piece of cultural programming most people have been exposed to. Even though the scientific literature does not support this idea, the programming remains. Your eating behavior up to this point may, in fact, have been driven primarily by your programming. Not only body image programming, of course, although that may be a significant part, but also programming about what food is for, what to eat, how and when to eat it. Cultures and families have a variety of idiosyncratic ideas about food, and much of your eating may reflect programming that you have never considered before. Before moving on, let's take a moment to consider this.

IDENTIFYING FOOD PROGRAMMING
The Past

1. What kinds of food did you eat when you were a child?

   _____
   _____
   _____
   _____
   _____
   _____

2. How were meals handled in your household growing up? How many meals a day did you have? What were they? Where and how did you eat them?

   _____
   _____
   _____
   _____

3. Were there special food traditions in your family? What did you eat on special occasions? Were there any cultural beliefs or traditions around food that your family practiced?

   _____
   _____

THE VALUE OF FEEDING YOURSELF

_____
_____
_____
_____

4. Do you have any negative memories surrounding food from childhood?

_____
_____
_____
_____
_____

5. Can you identify any programming that you are carrying around from your childhood experiences with food? What did you conclude about the way the world worked? What did you conclude about yourself? Have you formulated other rules based on this experience? Write down as many of these as you can identify.

_____
_____
_____
_____
_____
_____
_____
_____
_____
_____

The Present

6. What kinds of foods do you eat now?

_____
_____
_____
_____

7. How are meals handled in your household? How many meals a day do you eat? What are they? Where and how do you eat them? Is this different from how others who live with you eat? How?

8. Do you practice any special food traditions? How do you handle special meals or seasons, such as holidays?

9. Do you have any food secrets? Behaviors you engage in around food that cause negative emotion? What are these?

10. Can you identify any messages in your current eating patterns? What would someone from a different culture conclude about food, what is important, and how eating worked if they had you and your family as their only example? Write down as many ideas as you can.

_____
_____
_____
_____
_____
_____
_____
_____
_____
_____
_____
_____

What did you notice about your food programming past and present? One piece of programming you may have absorbed in our thin-ideal culture is the idea that "food is (or should be) fuel." But food, in every culture throughout human history, has never been simply fuel or calories to propel other activities. How and what we eat is rich with meaning. Food can provide nourishment or an opportunity to socialize. Food can serve as a vehicle for transmitting culture, defining gender or family roles, representing religious symbols, national or cultural identity. In this chapter, we will focus on food as a vehicle for awakening, for living the way you want to live. Foods represent an opportunity to live your values. What might that look like in your life?

FROM DIETS TO FOODWAYS

If you struggle with your body image, you may have been on many diets. The word "diet," like the word "fat," *can* be a neutral, non-judgmental word, referring to the kind of food a person habitually eats, for example, "John's diet consisted mainly of beans and ramen, with the occasional steak and potatoes." However, often the word diet means a restricted regimen of foods one is required to eat, either for medical reasons, or to lose weight. What do you think of when you hear the word diet? What role has this word played in your life?

_____
_____
_____
_____

The Health At Every Size (HAES) principle related to eating is called "Eating for Well-being," which means to "promote flexible, individualized eating based on hunger, satiety, nutritional needs, and pleasure, rather than any externally regulated eating plan focused on weight control." Weight loss dieting is not part of HAES, and is not part of the *Accept Yourself!* program. What does it mean to eat in a flexible, individualized way that is based on hunger, satiety, nutritional needs, and pleasure? Many people have spent so much time either on or falling off of a diet that this way of eating is difficult to imagine, and even more difficult to implement in practice. How can I tell if I'm hungry or full? How do I know what is nutritious? Is it OK to eat for pleasure, when I've been told my whole life that this is sinful and will make me gain weight?

Answering these questions may be part of a lifelong process for you as you recover from the harm that chronic dieting does. For now, however, we are going to sidestep the issues of hunger, fullness, and nutrition to consider all the reasons and ways people eat that are *not* related to simply fueling one's body adequately for health.

Anthropologists use the term "foodway" to describe a culture's "diet," that is, the way people in that culture habitually eat. The word "foodway" includes not only what foods are eaten, but also the rituals, meanings, and practices around food, in everyday life and on special occasions. We will be using the term "foodway" in this chapter as an alternative to the word "diet," both because "foodway" avoids the connotation of restriction, and also to highlight the many different functions and purposes food can serve in your life. In this book, we will define your "foodway" as a conscious way of eating that expresses your values and what is important to you.

The remainder of this chapter will involve exploring different foodways you may wish to explore. Food can be used to pursue all kinds of values apart from weight loss. What does this mean?

The table displays a variety of examples of values you might hold and wish to explore through food. For each value, you'll see some sample foodways (ways of eating) that might allow you to express those values, and also some resources and examples for how a person might follow that foodway, including blogs and websites that might serve as resources (or that represent an example of someone eating that foodway), as well as possible activities or exercises you could try in following that foodway.

Experimenting with Foodways

Values	Possible Foodways	Resources And Examples
Social justice, stronger communities, equality	Eating Fair Trade	www.fairtradeusa.org/blog Hosting a weekly or monthly Fair Trade neighborhood dinner, where only fairly traded foods are served. Buying as many Fair Trade foods as you can find instead of eating conventional alternatives.
	Supporting sustainable farms	www.sustainabletable.org Doing grocery shopping at farmer's markets. Asking farmers and food sellers about the details of how their foods are produced, and how to support them.
A better environment	Becoming a localvore	www.diaryofalocavore.com Doing the "eat local challenge," where, during the summer, you eat only foods grown or produced within 200 miles.
	Eating organic	http://livingmaxwell.com Swapping organic for conventional groceries. Shopping at stores that sell organic foods.
	Low-carbon eating (eating to prevent climate change)	www.eatlowcarbon.org Hosting a low-carbon-eating monthly or weekly dinner where friends eat a low-carbon meal and work on environmental issues. Having one meal a week be low carbon.

Values	Possible Foodways	Resources And Examples
Pleasure, joy, aesthetics, travel, adventure	Eating around the world	http://globaltableadventure.com Shopping at international grocery stores. Eating one meal a week from a different culture.
	Food as experiment	www.allenhemberger.com/alinea Asking chefs at your favorite restaurants to share recipes and recreating them at home. Trying a different restaurant or different food you have never tried each week. Cooking your way through a new cookbook. Documenting your meals on social media.
Spiritual growth, cultural identification	Keeping kosher	http://food.lizsteinberg.com Meeting with others at your synagogue to discuss the spiritual meaning of keeping kosher. Keeping kosher for a period of time (3 weeks? 6 months?) and noticing the effects.
	Eating halal	http://myhalalkitchen.com Shopping at halal markets. Discussing with family or friends at your mosque the spiritual value of halal. Making halal meals.
	Eating your culture's traditional foods	http://sioux-chef.com Visiting with elders to learn your culture's traditional food practices. Learning foraging, canning, and preserving. Growing a garden, making cheese, helping to butcher meat on a farm. Exploring your culture's traditional recipes.
Love, relationships	Eating adventurously what others offer	www.travelchannel.com/shows/bizarre-foods Accepting invitations to eat where before you turned them down. Eating what you are offered even if it doesn't fit with your tastes or your usual food practices.
	Cooking for loved ones	http://300sandwiches.com Making only one meal for your whole family where before you might eat special diet foods. Making a special "date meal" each week for a partner or child.
	Eating childhood comfort foods	http://biscuitsandsuch.com Cooking your way through a family cookbook. Creating a family cookbook. Meeting monthly or weekly with family members to recreate beloved childhood meals. Making and eating for yourself your favorite childhood comfort foods on a regular basis, as a form of self-care.

What Do You Want to Eat for?

What values (*apart* from those related to weight, shape, or health) would you like to explore through food? The table above gives examples, but they are by no means exhaustive. Pick one or two values you might like to explore with food:

_____

_____

_____

Now, what foodways might allow you to express those values in your eating? What kinds of experiments, challenges, or resources would you like to explore to express this value?

_____
_____
_____
_____
_____
_____

What can you commit to trying this week? When and how will you experiment with this foodway?

_____
_____
_____
_____
_____
_____

You've now had the chance to make several different kinds of changes in your eating patterns. In Chapter 3, you may have experimented with dietary changes designed to improve your health. In this chapter, now you have also experimented with using food to pursue other important values. Sometimes in the course of these explorations, people find that, in the absence of having to change your eating for your weight or your health, food is just *not that important*. Perhaps you didn't need to make a health change, and didn't find a foodway that spoke to you. Perhaps you did try to make a health change or a foodway change, but it didn't work to improve your health, didn't enhance your ability to live your values, or was too difficult to implement.

WHAT IF FOOD IS NOT SOMETHING I VALUE?

Not all people may have values they wish to express through food. Food, ultimately, is necessary for life, and a normal, healthy relationship with food leaves space for pursuing other values. But what is a "normal, healthy relationship with food?"

Nutritionist Ellyn Satter gives this excellent definition of normal eating:

> Normal eating is going to the table hungry and eating until you are satisfied. It is being able to choose food you like and eat it and truly get enough of it – not just stop eating because you think you should. Normal eating is being able to give some thought to your food selection so you get nutritious food, but not being so wary and restrictive that you miss out on enjoyable food. Normal eating is giving yourself permission to eat sometimes because you are happy, sad, or bored, or just because it feels good. Normal eating is mostly three meals a day, or four or five, or it can be choosing to munch along the way. It is leaving some cookies on the plate because you know you can have some again tomorrow, or it is eating more now because they taste so wonderful. Normal eating is overeating at times, feeling stuffed and uncomfortable. And it can be undereating at times and wishing you had more. Normal eating is trusting your body to make up for your mistakes in eating. Normal eating takes up some of your time and attention, but keeps its place as only one important area of your life. In

short, normal eating is flexible. It varies in response to your hunger, your schedule, your proximity to food and your feelings (Satter, 2008).

Notice that this definition isn't perfectionistic. There is plenty of room in this definition for many different foodways, ways of eating, and for plenty of variability in how you eat across a day or a year or many years. It's also worth noticing that this definition actively discourages a dogmatic, rules-based approach to eating.

What do you think of Satter's definition? Are you a normal eater according to this definition? In what ways are you engaging in normal eating now? In what ways does your eating not conform to this definition of normal eating? Take a few minutes and reflect here:

_____
_____
_____
_____
_____
_____
_____
_____
_____

You may already be practicing normal eating. However, if you have always dieted, or if you come from a family where many generations of women have always dieted, you may have *never* eaten in the way Ellyn Satter suggests. You may genuinely not know how to eat in this way. If you struggle with binge eating or other eating disorders or have a history of eating disorders, you may need professional help to achieve normal eating, and I encourage you to seek out a therapist who both practices Health At Every Size (HAES) principles and has expertise in treating eating disorders.

HOW DO I TELL IF I'M HUNGRY?

Some women have trouble with normal eating because they have trouble telling when they're hungry or full. If you have a long dieting history, or engage in binge eating or other eating disordered behaviors, this can be especially difficult. Professional help may be needed, and there are also several practices that can be helpful in beginning to understand your own hunger and fullness cues:

Mechanistic Eating

Mechanistic eating involves eating unrestricted quantities and types of food in a fashion that is organized and predictable (e.g., eating a specified number of meals and snacks at designated meal and snack times each day). It is not "normal eating," because it is highly structured, like a diet. It is not a diet, because weight loss is not a goal and foods are unrestricted. Mechanistic eating is a stepping stone to normal eating. It can help women stop binging and re-set their hunger cues so they become more predictable, and thus easier to observe. It should not be followed indefinitely, however, and it works best with professional help.

Nutritionist Marcia Herrin's food plan was written to help people recover from eating disorders, and it can be used for mechanistic eating. To follow Dr. Herrin's plan, you eat servings of food from a variety of food groups at three meals and three snacks throughout the day. In following this plan, it is a good idea to designate a window of time during which you will eat each meal or snack, and you agree to consume the meal or snack and not to eat outside of these six eating occasions during the day. Although Dr. Herrin gives a rough idea of serving sizes in her plan (she describes a serving as "usually one cup or twice the size listed on food labels"), and eating the specified food groups at the specified times does ensure eating a range of nutritious food, chronic dieters may be surprised by the lack of restriction in this mechanized eating plan. For example, "fun foods," such as desserts, cookies, cake, ice cream, chips, fries, and non-diet soda, can be eaten as often as five times a day on her plan. Nevertheless, even though this plan is not restrictive, it is important to emphasize that following it is *not* normal eating, and not an end in itself. Following a temporary mechanistic eating plan (ideally with professional help) is a stepping stone, a good place to start if you struggle with binging or identifying fullness and hunger. Following such a plan briefly helps your hunger and fullness cues to become more predictable, and thus perhaps more observable, but this is not a long-term plan for healthy eating. If you'd like to experiment with a brief trial of mechanistic eating, Dr. Herrin's plan is available here: www.eatingdisorderguides.com/HerrinFoodPlan.2013.pdf

Another way to help learn about your hunger and fullness cues is to use a hunger/fullness scale and journal to track and rate these cues. Nutritionist Karin Kratina has some sample scales and journals on her website here: www.eatingwisdom.com/eating-wisdom-products. Eating when you are physically hungry, stopping when you are full, and using internal body signals (not what you think you "should" eat) to gauge hunger and fullness, are associated with stable weight, normal eating, and improved body image. Using a hunger/fullness scale and journal can help you better observe your own hunger and fullness cues.

All of these practices may help you engage in normal eating if food is not a particular value in your life, and foodways may help you to use food as a forum for your values. Are there normal eating practices you'd like to experiment with this week? What are they, and when and how will you practice them?

_____

_____

_____

_____

_____

Letting go of dieting and the food programming related to it, and learning how to eat in service to what you really value some of the time, and to eat normally the rest of the time, can be frightening and challenging. Be gentle with yourself as you go through this experience. The most important aspect of normal eating to experiment with for now is flexibility. Food is never the only important value in your life, and if you have a history of chronic dieting, it may have taken a larger role than it should for many years, preventing you from doing other things you wanted and enjoyed, because you were too hungry, too ashamed and guilty, or too distracted thinking about food to focus on your passions. For that reason, I encourage you to experiment with the suggestions in this chapter, and then move on, even if you don't think you got them "right." Following a foodway and eating normally are not dogmas, and eating need not be governed by strict rules. Ideally, you are able to eat flexibly as the situation, your values, your wishes, your hunger and pleasure, and your nutritional needs demand. There's no right way or thing to eat, and no sin attached to eating. The only time to feel guilty about eating a food is if you stole it.

REFERENCES

Kornfield, J. (1994). *Buddha's little instruction book.* New York: Bantam.

Satter, E. (2008). *Secrets of feeding a healthy family: How to eat, how to raise good eaters, how to cook.* Madison, WI: Kelcy Press.

8
Embodying Your Values

Once again, before we discuss the topic of this chapter, how did your acceptance practices go this week? What did you do? What did you experience? Journal about your experiences here:

_____
_____
_____
_____
_____
_____
_____
_____
_____
_____

What will you do for your next acceptance practices? What is next on your list of painful situations? (Or would it be better to do your last acceptance exercise again, leaning in harder, before moving on?)

ACCEPTANCE PRACTICE #4

What I'll Do And How: _____

_____
_____
_____
_____
_____

When: _____

EMBODYING YOUR VALUES

We've explored how eating can reflect your programming, the rules you've been taught about what you are "allowed" to eat, what is moral, appropriate, or healthful for you to eat (and what isn't). You may have similar programming related to what you are allowed to do with your body, both how and where you are allowed to enjoy your body and make use of its abilities, and also how you are allowed to adorn your body. Betsy, for example, carried a piece of programming that said her fat body was "disgusting" to touch, and thus, although she wanted to get a professional massage, she never had. Ellora was willing to run on her treadmill in her women's-only gym, but carried programming that she should not run in her workout clothes in public (and she had also experienced fat-shaming discrimination when she had tried). Lindsay had been told she couldn't wear bright colors, horizontal stripes, or long hair, because these weren't "flattering."

What about you? What kind of programming are you carrying about your body, and how you can adorn it or use it? Are you "allowed" to wear tank tops, horizontal stripes, short hair, fashionable clothes, bright colors, body conscious, "skimpy," or revealing lingerie, swimwear, or other fashion? Are there things you are "allowed" or "not allowed" to do with your hair or makeup? Have you experienced any discrimination for "breaking" these rules? What did you make of that? Reflect on these questions here.

_____

_____

_____

_____

_____

What about physical activities or sensual experiences, things you can do with your body. Are there activities you are not "allowed" to do because of your size or shape or weight? Are there sexual or romantic experiences you avoid because of programming, fears, or discrimination? Have you had difficulty finding a partner, or experienced abuse from a partner, for reasons that someone may have tried to tie to your size or shape? What about travel? Physical activities? Can you do some things in one context or time, but not another? Have you experienced any discrimination for "breaking" these rules? Reflect on these questions here.

_____

_____

_____

_____

_____

Physical appearance and physical activity can reflect your programming. You may be very aware of how hemmed in you are by rules or beliefs you picked up along the way about how bodies like yours could look, what they could do, where they could go, and you may also have had difficult or traumatic experiences of discrimination when you broke the "rules." But physical appearance and activity, like food, can also be used *creatively* as a means of displaying or promoting values or producing your own programming. The goal of this chapter is to help you experiment with values-driven aspects of your appearance and self-presentation. The next chapter will discuss values-driven activities in more detail.

FASHION WITHOUT SELF-HATRED: HOW?

Journalist Tanya Gold, in a 2010 article for the *Guardian*, which you can read online here: www.theguardian.com/lifeandstyle/2010/jan/22/i-hate-fashion-tanya-gold, described her hatred of fashion. She discussed how she acquired fashion programming that told her she was not enough: "I discovered fashion when I was 13. Before that I dressed as Andy Pandy and was very happy. No one sticks Andy Pandy in 6 inch heels to emphasize the sexual organs he doesn't have." She described how giving up Andy Pandy and dressing as she was "supposed" to didn't make her feel better. Instead, she felt more insecure, less attractive, and always "too fat." She noted that fashion seemed to stoke the insecurities of even professionally beautiful women. She had interviewed cover models for *Vogue* and noted that they too shared her feelings of inadequacy and lack of worthiness when they tried to look beautiful or be fashionable. What do you think? Do you agree with Ms. Gold? Can you relate to her experience?

Fashion blogger Tavi Gevinson, who was then just 14 years old, did not. (You can read her counterpoint in full here: www.thestylerookie.com/2010/01/fashion-basically-also-team-conan.html) She noted that fashion is a creative, artistic industry, and that many possible values can be explored through clothing, not just the programming of being feminine and physically attractive: "I find the idea of dressing as Andy Pandy pretty awesome. It's creative and it's fun, and that sounds fashionable to me. What Tanya Gold and many others, including myself, hate is the everyone-has-to-look-the-same-and-also-sexy philosophy, which is *not* fashion."

What might fashion without self-hatred look like? Could Tanya Gold have gone on wearing striped pajamas and a matching striped hat, like Andy Pandy, if she wanted to? How might you look or dress if you could look any way you wanted to, and if you also did not have to worry about conforming to any particular rules about your appearance, if you could wear whatever you wished and not be judged?

Sakina, a fat woman and artistic director for a non-profit organization, dressed carefully, in the most fashionable designer labels she could find in her size, with time-consuming makeup, and a top-of-the-line salon maintaining her hair. She spent more of her budget on her appearance than she could really afford, so it might surprise you to learn that her answer was: "I'd wear sloppy sweatsuits and no makeup at all, every day. I'd wear my hair in a ponytail all the time." Sakina noted that her careful appearance was her way to avoid size-based and racial discrimination and to make sure the organization she directed was not negatively affected by her "sloppiness," which was the programming she carried related to the meaning of her body size. She longed for the opportunity not to have to care about fashion or self-presentation, and instead focus on the creative activities of her organization.

Jodie, however, a New Yorker who worked in the service industry, laughed: "I'd probably spend my whole paycheck on Fifth Avenue, and then some, if they had anything on the whole street that I could fit." Carolyn, a stay-at-home parent, wished that she could dye her hair "galaxy," bright purple and blue hair colors to look like the night sky. Allysen, who worked for a non-profit organization, said that she would wear tight and revealing workout wear.

What about you? What's your answer to this question? How might *you* look or dress if you could look any way you wanted to, and if you also did not have to worry about conforming to any particular rules about your appearance, if you could wear whatever you wished and not be judged?

_____

_____

_____

_____

_____

_____

What about your appearance-related values? Apart from physical appearance or attractiveness or conformity, what do you want to dress for? In other words, if you already and always looked exactly as you most would wish and were perceived exactly as you would hope others would see you, no matter what you wore or did to your appearance, what values would you want your physical appearance to serve?

It's a somewhat strange and complicated question, isn't it? Just as with the foodways we explored in the last chapter, there are a variety of values you might hold and wish to explore through self-presentation and physical appearance. To help you picture them and answer this question for yourself, we'll explore several example values you could express in your appearance, again using a table. For each one, you'll see a brief example of someone who is (at least in part) wearing this values-driven self-presentation, and also some resources and experiments and activities you could try if you wanted to explore that value too.

Values-Driven Self-Presentations

Valued Self-Presentation	Example	Resources And Ideas
Wearing your culture's traditional dress	Samah Salaime, a Palestinian woman who keeps Palestinian clothing traditions alive, with writing, a non-profit that helps crafters sell their work, and a unique photo project, where Palestinian women activists wear their traditional clothes. Read more about Samah here: https://972mag.com/how-palestinian-women-are-enlisting-traditional-dresses-into-the-struggle/117802	Research traditional and modern dress for your state, region, nationality, heritage nationalities, ethnicity, and religion. Wear a traditional costume at a special event or cultural celebration. Wear an accessory with cultural significance as part of your outfit. Have a traditional garment custom made for you.
Simple dress	Sheena Matheiken created the Uniform Project. She wore the same dress every day for a year, styling it artistically each day and posting pictures to raise money for the Akansha Foundation, which educates impoverished Indian children. Read more about Sheena here: www.theuniformproject.com	Create your own Uniform Project, wearing the same outfit daily and making it your own with accessories and styling. Try Labour Behind the Label's Six Items Challenge, where you choose six clothing items to wear for six weeks. Read more about the challenge here: http://labourbehindthelabel.org/get-involved/fundraise-for-us/the-six-items-challenge

Valued Self-Presentation	Example	Resources And Ideas
		Use simple dressing to raise money for an organization you care about or showcase your creativity through social media.
DIY and handmade fashion	Mary Alice Duff began to sew when she found it challenging to find stylish, well-fitting clothes in her size. Her sewing blog, Well Sewn Style, allows her to express her creativity and tailoring skills. Read Well Sewn Style here: www.wellsewnstyle.com	Try a variety of 10-minute or 30-minute sewing projects online. Some examples: http://crazylittleprojects.com/2014/08/quickandeasysewingprojects.html www.sewmyplace.com/project/150-sewing-projects Learn to sew for a fat body from plus-size tutorials, patterns, and communities. For example: The Curvy Sewing Collective, http://curvysewingcollective.com Refashion an existing piece of clothing, by modifying it to suit yourself. You can find some tutorials for plus-size refashion at One Brown Mom (www.onebrownmom.com) and the Refashion Co-Op (http://refashionco-op.blogspot.com). Design your clothes without sewing using online custom retailers. For example, Impish Lee (http://impishlee.com) sells lingerie in sizes up to 24 (bottoms) and 40J (bras), which you design with fabrics, trims, and styles of your choice.
Outfit blogging and creating trends	Search social media and Instagram hashtags such as #effyourbeautystandards, #fashionforwardplus, #whatfatgirlsactuallywear, #fatshion, #fatbabe, #wewearwhatwewant, #volup2isdiversity, #plussizefashion, #plusisequal, and #psootd (plus-size outfit of the day) to see examples of people of all sizes expressing values through clothing.	Try a daily outfit blogging challenge, taking a daily selfie of your outfit or some aspect of your self-presentation (makeup, shoes, hair, accessories), and then upload it to social media using one of these or other hashtags to connect with like-minded communities. Using hashtags, identify one way to wear current fashion trends you'd like to try. Consider how you want to respond to discrimination or abusive behavior online. Would you prefer to have a private social media account? Do you want to make your photos public to support other women? How do you want to respond to online abuse if it occurs?
Wearing eco-chic (environmentally friendly or ethically produced) clothing	Singer Beth Ditto created a fashion line that features edgy, fashion-forward clothing in a variety of cuts up to 3X and that is sewn by artisans in New York City (https://shop.bethditto.com).	Invest in a piece of eco-friendly or ethically produced clothing from Beth Ditto's line or one of these resources: Lur Clothing makes eco-friendly, natural and recycled-fiber clothing, in sizes up to 24 (http://lurapparel.com).

Valued Self-Presentation	Example	Resources And Ideas
		Kobomo is an Australian, Bohemian-style brand that uses a charitable buying structure, and has sizes up to up to 3X (https://kobomo.com.au/collections/plus-sizes). Eileen Fisher makes classic, tailored clothes using mostly organic materials and eco-friendly production methods, with a plus line that goes up to 3X (www.eileenfisher.com/shop/size/plus). Decent Exposures makes underwear, activewear, swimwear, and a made-to-measure "un bra" in Seattle, out of organic fibers, in sizes up to 4X (with unlimited custom sizing for the un bra; https://decentexposures.com). Zero Waste designer Daniel Silverstein will customize his line for an affordable add-on to his regular prices to accommodate people of all sizes (http://zerowastedaniel.com/custom). Sara Laughed has a comprehensive spreadsheet of ethical and eco-friendly plus brands: http://saralaughed.com/fair-trade-plus-size-ethical-clothing
Culture jamming	Author Jes Baker read that former Abercrombie and Fitch CEO, Mike Jeffries, commented that Abercrombie & Fitch (A&F) did not want unattractive or unpopular people wearing their brand. (A&F does not carry sizes above a 10). Jes, a fat women, got a large A&F t-shirt and wore it to an "Attractive & Fat" photoshoot in the style of A&F ads. Baker has called this an example of "culture jamming:" creating alternative images to challenge cultural programming.	Look at some of Jes Baker's culture jamming photoshoots: www.themilitantbaker.com/2013/05/to-mike-jeffries-co-abercrombie-fitch.html www.themilitantbaker.com/2013/12/lustworthy-statement-for-visible-woman.html www.themilitantbaker.com/2014/02/lustworthy-this-is-truth-from-jl.html Listen to Jes talk about culture jamming on the *Body Kindness* podcast: www.bodykindnessbook.com/2017/04/12/podcast-27-culture-jamming-mindful-healing-jes-baker Wear a provocative, political or artistic t-shirt. Have a custom t-shirt made with a slogan or design that expresses your own values.

Valued Self-Presentation	Example	Resources And Ideas
Living publicly while fat	Remember Sakina from the beginning of the chapter, who longed to be free of careful attention to fashion? She began to wear "sloppy sweats" and t-shirts on weekends and to go to work without makeup or hair color. Her goal was to express the value that she did not have to adhere to beauty standards.	Give yourself permission to wear whatever clothes are currently off limits to you because of size. Try investing less attention in your appearance, and experimenting with other ways of standing up against size-based discrimination and abuse.

What kind of values-driven self-presentation would you like to try? On the next page, you have space to draw, journal, or paste in images that express how you want to wear or adorn yourself in your values.

MY VALUES-DRIVEN SELF-PRESENTATION

The Bathing Suit Exercise

Whatever your values-driven self-presentation, learning to living (more) publicly while fat (or average-sized, or thin, or tall, or short, etc.) is an opportunity to create space for other values. One way to experiment with this is the *bathing suit exercise*. Many women are either not "allowed" to wear swimwear at all based on body-shaming programming, or experience intense discomfort related to swimwear. Is this true for you? Do you have a bathing suit in your current size? When was the last time you wore it? How does the idea of wearing it out to a pool or beach, or changing into it in a locker room, feel to you? Are there circumstances that would make this easier or more difficult? Going to a particular beach or pool? Going alone or with others? Changing in the open in a locker room versus in a stall or shower? Lying by the pool where you might be visible to others versus staying as much time as possible in the water? Simply going to try on bathing suits at all? Simply wearing a suit in your own home? Even if you feel very comfortable in your bathing suit, are there bathing suit-related situations that might bring up body shame and discomfort? Wearing a sexy or revealing suit? Wearing a two piece? Doing a photoshoot in a swimsuit? For this exercise, identify a bathing-suit-related activity that is definitely uncomfortable, and engage in it. If you do not have a bathing suit, Love Your Peaches (www.loveyourpeaches.com) sells made-in-America swimwear in custom (unlimited) sizing, and uses models of diverse sizes in their marketing materials. Swimsuits for All (www.swimsuitsforall.com/Plus-Size-Swimwear) has fashion-forward options in sizes 4–34. What uncomfortable-but-courageous bathing suit activity will you try for this exercise?

_____

_____

_____

When will you do it? What will you need to do or prepare to do it? (Swimsuit? Supportive friends? Directions to the beach?)

_____

_____

_____

_____

Fashion Without Self-Hatred: Resources

Whatever your size or shape or values, if you enjoy fashion and self-adornment, you deserve beautiful clothing that flatters your figure. Finding fashion to fit larger bodies can be challenging. Sometimes the clothes that are available appear designed to harm your self-esteem, another form of size discrimination. Sharing resources helps us find and reward retailers that make beautiful clothing.

We've looked at several retailers in this chapter already, but here are some other shopping resources that offer fashionable, fun clothes in a wide range of sizes.

- Monif C (plus-size fashion, especially swimwear): http://monifc.com
- Jessica Louise (trendy, fashion-forward, less-expensive clothing): www.shopjessicalouise.com/collections/plus-sizing
- ModCloth Plus Size: www.modcloth.com (sizes from XXS to 4X across the line)
- Asos Curve (known for button-up shirts that will fit large bustlines, as well as other clothes): http://us.asos.com/women/curve-plus-size/cat/?cid=9577
- Torrid: www.torrid.com/torrid/Homepage.jsp

- We Love Colors has cute plus-size tights: www.welovecolors.com/Shop/PlusSizedHosiery.htm
- Forever 21 Plus Size: www.forever21.com/Product/Category.aspx?br=plus&category=plus_main
- Figleaves has cute lingerie in a range of sizes: www.figleaves.com/us
- Junonia has plus-size activewear: www.junonia.com
- Igigi has pretty plus-size dresses: www.igigi.com
- EShakti has gorgeous, custom clothes in any size: www.eshakti.com
- Addition Elle's tagline is "Believe in fashion democracy:" www.additionelle.com
- Simply Be (party dresses, designer clothes): www.simplybe.com
- Gwynnie Bee rents designer clothing up to size 32: https://closet.gwynniebee.com
- Premme (designer clothes in sizes 12–30, priced from $30 to $89): www.premme.us

Blogs, Tumblr, Instagram, Pinterest, and YouTube channels can provide additional resources, community, and visual inspiration. Here are some to start with:

- The political blog Shakesville hosts an occasional Fat Fashion thread where larger women can share resources, tips, photos, and product recommendations: www.shakesville.com/search/label/Fat%20Fashion
- Ravings by Rae, Chicago-based fashion blog and YouTube channel: http://ravingsbyrae.com
- Migg Mag (international vintage style): www.miggmag.com
- Kelly Augustine, New York fashion blogger: www.kellyaugustine.com
- Chante blogs about size acceptance via fashion at Everything Curvy and Chic: www.everythingcurvyandchic.com
- Fashion To Figure (both a blog and a store): www.fashiontofigure.com/blog
- Tess Holliday, first size 22 supermodel signed to a major agency: www.tessholliday.com
- 22+ Blogger Lookbook, featuring plus size fashion bloggers in favorite outfits: https://issuu.com/fearlesslyjustme/docs/style_22__blogger_lookbook_-_fall_2?reader3=1

Surprising Your Mirror

This chapter has offered a variety of experiences for experimenting with bold, visible, and courageous self-presentation. Self-adornment, like cuisine, is a unique human universal, which may have been used to hurt you. This program offers you an opportunity to reclaim self-adornment in your own, bold, creative way, if you want that. There is an element of acceptance in engaging in self-presentation experiments. If you try a boldly visible hairstyle, bright, fanciful makeup, a political t-shirt, a selfie on social media, to wear a tank top to the gym or store, you may feel ashamed, ugly, or unacceptable. These experiences call for acceptance (not control), as well as courage. You have the right to wear whatever you want, even if it's uncomfortable. You have the right to play with sexuality, attractiveness, rejection of beauty standards, and artistic expression with your appearance, and this right is not dependent on your size or shape or self-image. (This right is also not dependent on how others respond. If you are responded to with discrimination, that is not your fault.) What final exercise would you like to try in this chapter to creatively program and challenge your ideas of how you "should" or can look? Do you want to try carnival-colored hair? A glittery eyeliner? A pin-up-style bikini? A tank top with bare arms? Platform boots? To skip makeup at work? A political t-shirt? Identify an exercise that both fits your values and feels daring, frightening, surprising, and write it here:

_____

_____

_____

_____

When and how will you commit to surprising your mirror in this way? Make your commitment here, then carry it out:

_____

_____

_____

_____

9
Dancing with Your Body to the Life You Really Want

One last time, before we discuss the topic of this chapter, how did your acceptance practices go this week? What did you do? What did you experience? Journal about your experiences here:

_____
_____
_____
_____
_____
_____
_____
_____
_____

What will you do for your next acceptance practices? What is next on your list of painful situations?

ACCEPTANCE PRACTICE #5

What I'll Do And How: _____
_____
_____
_____
_____
_____

When: _____

DANCING WITH YOUR BODY TO THE LIFE YOU REALLY WANT
Imagine you somehow find yourself in this situation: You open the mail to an elegant invitation from the unknown friend of your dearest childhood pal: A bachelorette party in Las Vegas, with all the perks

included. She mentions free admission to all the newest, hottest nightclubs, where you, the bride, and all her other friends – most of whom you've never met – will dance all night long. During the day, they've reserved a poolside cabana at a luxurious resort hotel. It won't cost you a dime; even your airline tickets are in the envelope.

An all-expense-paid trip with your dearest old friend and no luxury spared: Is this a dream come true? Or has your mind already conjured up the nightmare? The bride's skinny, adorable friends will be judgmental and critical. You have nothing to wear to a nightclub. You'll look ridiculous on the dance floor. And how on earth can you get out of the afternoon at the pool and cabana? Even if you had a bathing suit, there's no chance you'd risk wearing it at a luxury resort. Surely you can just see your friend at the wedding, you think, as you leave a message on the hostess's voicemail with the best excuse you can conjure up for turning down a free vacation.

Take a moment and jot down how you would react if you received such an invitation. (If you don't feel the situation applies to you, jot down some notes about how you would feel if the opportunity arose to do any exciting activity that would nevertheless put your body and food choices on public display.)

_____

_____

_____

_____

_____

Kate Harding, a writer who blogs about body image and self acceptance, was lucky enough to receive such an invitation, and in her essay "Bachelorettes and Bathing Suits" (which you can read here: http://kateharding.net/2009/04/10/bachelorettes-bathing-suits-etc) she described both the dream and the nightmare involved. She discusses the urge to cancel, the stress over what to wear, how she would look, and whether an unknown group of adult women friends might judge her. But Harding decided to go to the party anyway. She describes how, in the past, she would have decided to skip the whole thing, out of fears that she would be the fattest person at the party (which she was), and that her friends or friends-of-friends would be humiliated and disgusted by the sight of her. But, as she stated, "And the thing is, none of that would have been true then, either. But I never would have found out the fears were bullshit. I never would have found out that flitting between a cabana and an enormous pool all afternoon is pretty much my idea of heaven."

In the previous pages of this book, you have learned the basic skills of self-acceptance and mindful, non-judgmental, observation of yourself and your body. You have practiced using these skills to reinvent your appearance, style, and your relationship to food, based on your values and dreams, and not on your fears. If you've completed these exercises, congratulations: You now own the swimsuit, you've worn it outdoors, and you've begun to develop the bikini-ready mind that allows you to wear it with, if not confidence, at least a sense of righteousness. You are – all of you – allowed to be here. So now what?

Now that you have the skills, and the evidence of your own experience, to attest to your basic right to eat and move and dress in ways that make your dreams and values visible, rather than invisible, the job of this last chapter is to remind you what your own idea of heaven is, and to help you move towards that in the days, weeks, and years that will follow. This chapter is designed to help you see and appreciate your body and your life for what it is: your vehicle for awakening, your resource to draw upon to carry you towards the life you want.

Even though she made her living advocating for body image self-acceptance for people of all sizes, when it came to attending her friend's bachelorette party, Harding didn't pack effortless self-confidence in her bags. Instead, she carried fears: of being seen in public in a swimsuit, of being judged by others, of being hounded for her food choices or her appearance. Yet she used these feared-but-valued activities of swimming, dancing, and supporting a dear friend in her marriage as forums to demonstrate her commitment to friendship, self-acceptance, and joy. Living a valued life takes courage. It is your task, in this final chapter, to begin to pursue your deepest dreams and values courageously.

BARRIERS TO YOUR VALUES

At this point in your journey, you have learned, from experience, a great deal about your body, your mind, and how the two interact. Take a moment and turn back to Chapter 3, to the magic wand exercise, where you envisioned your "perfect body" fantasy, and the exercises that followed it where you clarified your dreams and values. Look at them again. Have they shifted? You'll see that the page is reprinted here, so you can take some time now to revise them so they reflect the person you are now, the changes you have made in your life since beginning this program, and any other changes that you wish to make.

CAN YOU LIVE THE LIFE YOU'VE ALWAYS WANTED?

The Magic Wand Revisited

Your Dreams

- _____
- _____
- _____
- _____
- _____
- _____
- _____
- _____
- _____
- _____
- _____
- _____
- _____
- _____
- _____
- _____
- _____
- _____
- _____
- _____
- _____
- _____
- _____
- _____
- _____
- _____
- _____
- _____

Your Values (Why Is This Important?)

- _____
- _____
- _____
- _____
- _____
- _____
- _____
- _____
- _____
- _____
- _____
- _____
- _____
- _____
- _____
- _____
- _____
- _____
- _____
- _____
- _____
- _____
- _____
- _____
- _____
- _____
- _____
- _____

The dreams you've written here are your road map for the future; while the values will provide a guiding compass if you ever get lost. They are important, so I hope you will polish them until they truly reflect who you are and what you want out of life. At the same time, be aware that your dreams, especially, are likely to change and evolve; they may be different in a decade, or a year, or even as soon as next week. They can be changed or discarded at any time. In the meantime they provide a place to begin.

Now is the time: Go out and pursue your values. Achieve your dreams! There's no time to waste, so please set down the book now and begin immediately.

So: Did you do that? Have you become the person you truly wanted to be since reading the above paragraph? Have you achieved your most important goals, your fondest dreams? Perhaps not? (Or at least, not entirely?)

What happened instead? Write down exactly what your mind gave you, and what you did (if anything), immediately after reading the previous page. (No cheating. Really, write down *exactly* what happened.)

_____

_____

_____

_____

_____

When I give this suggestion to my patients; ask them in the midst of a session, or perhaps at the end, as they are leaving my office, to go out and achieve their dreams *right now*, generally the only thing that actually happens *immediately* is that their minds produce, and they immediately explain to me, all the reasons why pursuing their dreams and values today is impossible. Did your mind do the same thing? If it did, wonderful! Thank it; that's exactly what our minds often do. (Mine does this, too.)

Those reasons, all that work your mind just did: Those things are *your barriers*. Barriers are everywhere. When you set out with great courage and willingness and excitement to achieve your dreams and pursue your values, chances are you will not take even one step before a barrier emerges to stop you.

Most often – although not always – this barrier is internal. It may be an emotion:

- Fear of the unknown or what others will think.
- Shame in response to the pride the dream invoked.
- Depression at the overwhelming nature of the tasks required of you now.

It may be a thought:

- "I want to start a dance school, but I'd have to rent a studio, and I'm broke and in debt."
- "I'd like to be a loving partner, but no one has ever loved this fat body, and no one ever will."
- "Maybe when I lose 50 lbs, I can take the chance and try interviewing for that TV job. I'd never get it in the shape I'm in now."

Other times, the initial barrier may be external. Many barriers that you may *perceive* as external are actually, at least at the time they first stand in your way, internal barriers. For example, it may be true that one needs to rent a dance studio before starting a dance school, or that that specific TV job discriminates, and would not hire a fat person, but these barriers do not appear and stop progress after you've interviewed at the TV station or signed up a classroom full of dance pupils. They are imagined futures that stop forward progress before the first steps have even been taken. External barriers do arise, however: One woman I worked with, for example, developed the courage to apply for a grant for her artwork, and when she went to the organization website to download the grant application, she discovered that funding for the program had been cut and the grant program no longer existed.

Imagine yourself walking on a path towards what really matters to you. Your values are the guiding stars you are following: No matter where the path leads, you can follow them. Your dreams and goals are a castle at the end of the path: They are where you are ultimately headed. Your barriers – both internal and external – represent a huge brick wall blocking your way to the castle and your view of the stars. Most people respond to that brick wall by backing up and looking for a way around, or a different path entirely, one with no brick walls. When they can't find one, they conclude that either their dream is impossible or that their approach is fatally flawed. Most people think barriers are the sign that they are doing something wrong. But here's the difficulty with that: It is the very act of moving towards your dreams and values that brings up barriers. By pursuing your dreams and values with full effort and attention, not only are you not avoiding barriers, you are actually *guaranteeing* that barriers will emerge for you.

If you don't believe me, consider for a moment any one of your heroes. Who is a public figure whose life and work you admire? Put their name and picture below, and take some time to research their biography and write some notes about it here. Pay particular attention to barriers your hero faced on his or her path to greatness. You'll discover – no matter whom you picked! – that your hero faced so many serious problems on his or her path to greatness that you would understand perfectly if she or he had given up and sunk into obscurity. But that isn't what happened. Instead, your hero used his or her problems and barriers as a forum to achieve great things and live a valued life. Is this true for your hero?

My Hero

[Paste a picture of your hero here.]

My hero's barriers:

_____
_____
_____
_____
_____

Now that you've considered the obstacles faced by someone you admire, what about your own barriers, both internal and external? When you look at the dreams and values you identified in Chapter 3 and revised earlier, what stands in your way? On the next page, make a list of these. Include both any concrete external barriers that stand in your way, and also all the emotions, thoughts, and doubts that stop you from moving forwards.

My Barriers

- _____
- _____
- _____
- _____
- _____
- _____
- _____
- _____
- _____
- _____
- _____
- _____
- _____
- _____
- _____
- _____
- _____
- _____
- _____
- _____
- _____
- _____
- _____
- _____
- _____
- _____
- _____
- _____
- _____
- _____

With internal barriers, such as thoughts, memories, or visions of the future, efforts to talk back to them, to get rid of them, to be "rational" about them, are like efforts to turn away from the brick wall in your path. They go nowhere, and in the meantime, you are engaged in a fruitless struggle to "feel better" before you can act. Instead, you might try bringing your fears along with you, willingly holding them inside of you as you move towards what really matters. You tried this in Chapter 8, with the bathing suit exercise, when you took negative feelings with you for a day at the beach or the pool. Now consider, where else could you go if you could easily bring these thoughts and feelings along for the ride?

_____

_____

_____

_____

_____

THE MAGIC WAND REVISITED

As you've worked through the exercises of this chapter, you've had several opportunities to reflect on where you started when you first began this journey: With a wave of a magic wand to give you the life you've always dreamed of. When you began this book, you may have wondered if you could ever have that, if you could ever become the person you truly wanted to be in the body you have now.

Where are you with that belief now? Has it shifted? Take a few moments and jot some notes to reflect upon the work you've done here and the progress you've made. What has changed in your life? With your body image? With your eating, dressing, and physical activity? With your commitment to your values and dreams? How did you get here from there? What were the most important changes you made and experiences you had as you went along?

_____

_____

_____

_____

_____

The answers to these questions are your resources for the future. The fact that you have made changes is admirable: I salute you for your hard work! The way you were able to make those changes – the things you did to help yourself grow – are the paths you can return to in the future when the going gets tough, when barriers emerge that you are unsure how to climb or absorb.

Look once more at your revised values and dreams on page 88. Are there any more changes or revisions you need to make now? Make them, again, once more. You will make and remake this road map many times in the future. Now ask yourself: What's next? What are the steps, both large and small, that you can take now that will move you closer? What barriers stand in your way? You may wish to use art and/or writing on the next page to consider and commit to your next steps. I am confident that the world needs more of what is contained in your fondest dreams and your most deeply held values, so I encourage you to bring the barriers along on your journey and see what you can do with them. Your body and mind, your heart and soul, just as they are today, are your vehicles to achieve greatness.

My Next Steps

CONGRATULATIONS ON YOUR VALUED LIFE!

You have made it to the end of this journey – or perhaps you have only just begun! Even without having had the privilege of meeting you yet, I am proud of you for what you have accomplished, and impressed with your hard work and determination to get here. The seeds of greatness are contained within each of us, and I have felt truly honored and lucky to have had the opportunity to be helpful to you as you take steps towards a better world. I'd also be thrilled to hear about the steps along your journey. You can reach me via email at margit.i.berman@dartmouth.edu (put "*Accept Yourself!* reader question" on your subject line for best results), or at my website at https://margitberman.com. Once again, congratulations! Let me wave that magic wand once more and share my final three wishes for you:

1. I wish you genuine appreciation for your wonderful and amazing body.
2. I wish for you a feast of delicious foods and a closet full of elegant adornments that all serve your values.
3. And, finally, I wish for you the opportunity to achieve whatever it is you dream of most and to become the kind of person who have always wanted to be, with many instructive brick walls and even more loving support along the way to strengthen your resolve.

All the best to you. Do keep in touch.

Index

22+ Blogger Lookbook 83
300 Sandwiches 69

acceptance 33, 46, 56–58, 83; body-image related 50; food-related 50; and painful situations 49–52; weekly practices 54–56, 63, 74, 85
accuracy of body image 44–45
Addition Elle 83
Akansha Foundation **77**
Alinea Project, The **69**
Albers, Susan 58
animals' response to dietary restriction 14
Aphramor, Lucy 59
artist's viewpoint for mindfulness 45
Asos Curve 82
Association for Contextual Behavioral Science 59
Association for Size Diversity and Health 25–26, 57; find-a-provider tool 26
Augustine, Kelly 83
avoidance 49; in the midst of acceptance 53

bad moods *see* negative moods
Bacon, Linda 57–59
Baker, Jes 59, **79**
barriers 21, 30, 87–88; external 23, 90–92; internal 23, 90–92, 94
bathing suit *see* swimsuit
bikini *see* swimsuit
binging 14–15, 50, 59, 71–72
Biscuits and Such **69**
Bizarre Foods **69**
Blank, Hanne 58–59
blood glucose 26, 28, 32
blood pressure 16, 25–26, 28, 32, 56
body-disparagement-free zone 58, 60
body dissatisfaction 7
Body Impolitic 59
Body Kindness **79**
body mass index (BMI) 15, 17; and mortality risk 15–16
Body Positive 59
brick walls 90–91, 96
Buddhism 61
Burgard, Deb 58–59

Café Liz **69**
Campos, Paul 59
casino metaphor 11
castle on the hill metaphor 20, 90
Chante 83
Chastain, Ragen 57, 59
chatter 41, 48, 55, 57–58
cholesterol 25–26, 28, 32
compass metaphor 20–21, 23, 89
costs of your problem 3–5
Curvy Sewing Collective, The **78**
culture jamming **79**

Dances with Fat 59
dangerous thoughts 36, 47–48
Decent Exposures **79**
defused bombs 47–49
defusion 47–49
discrimination 20, 23, 56–58, **78**, **80**; from medical providers 25–26, 28, 56–57; and physical appearance 75, 82–83; and physical health 17, 25–26, 59; racial 25, 76
Ditto, Beth **78**
DIY fashion **78**
dreams 3, 22, *24*, 43, 58, 86–89, 94; and barriers 90–92; case examples 20–21, 23
Duff, Mary Alice **78**
DuFrene, Troy 59

Eat Local Challenge **68**
eating disorders 7, 15, 71
eco-chic clothing **78**
Edison, Laurie Toby 59
Eifert, Georg 5, 7
Eileen Fisher **79**
Ellis, Albert 40
EShakti 83
exercise *see* physical activities
Everything Curvy and Chic 83

fashion 7, 59, 75–84
Fashion to Figure 83
The Fat Nutritionist 59
Figleaves 83
Folklore of Sex, The 40

INDEX

"food is fuel" 67
foodways 67–72; comfort foods **69**; cooking for loved ones **69**; eating for pleasure 25, 68, **69**, 72; Fair Trade **68**; halal **69**; kosher **69**; localvore **68**; love and relationships **69**; low-carbon **68**; sustainable farms **68**; traditional foods **69**; travel **69**
Forever 21 Plus Size 83
Frankel, Ellen 59
Free Mindfulness Project 46
Full Belly, The 59
"fun foods" 72

Gevinson, Tavi 76
Gold, Tanya 76
guilt/shame foods **50**
Gwynnie Bee 83

hair 75–76, **78**, **80**, 83
handmade fashion *see* DIY fashion
Harding, Kate 19, 59, 86–87
hashtags **78**
Hayes, Steven 58
Health At Every Size (HAES) 25, 58; Community 57; principles 25, 67–68, 71
health change goals 29–32
health screenings 26, 28–29, 32
Heffner, Michelle 5, 7
Herrin, Marcia 71–72
Holliday, Tess 83
hunger cues 71–72
hunger/fullness scale and journal 72
hypertension *see* blood pressure

Igigi 83
Impish Lee **78**
intentional weight loss 16
Iron Fat 59

Jessica Louise 82
Junonia 83

Kirby, Marianne 59
Kobomo **79**
Kollak, Ingrid 58
Kratina, Karin 72

Labour Behind the Label **77**
Lessons from the Fat-O-Sphere 59
Linehan, Marsha 46–47
Living Maxwell **68**
living publicly while fat **80**
loving your body 49
Lur Clothing **78**

magic wand fantasy 19–21, 23, 58, 63, 87–88, 94, 96; and physical activity 41–42
makeup 75–76, **78**, **80**, 83
map metaphor 20, 23, *24*, 89, 94

Matheiken, Sheena **77**
Matz, Judith 59
May, Michelle 59
mechanistic eating 71–72
medical care 26–28, 57
Migg Mag 83
Militant Baker, The 59
mindful movement 46, 49
mindfulness 46–49; meditation 46, 49; practice 44–47, 49
Minnesota Semi-Starvation Study 14–15
ModCloth Plus Size 82
Monif C 82
mountain metaphor for acceptance 52–53, 55
My Halal Kitchen **69**

National Institutes of Health 14
negative moods 15, 49–50, 51
normal eating 70–72
Notkin, Debbie 59

obesity 13–17, 25–26
obesity paradox 16
Oliver, J. Eric 59
One Brown Mom **78**
Orwell, George 40, 43
outfit blogging **78**

physical activities 25, 28, 46, 58, 75, 94
physical appearance 77–84
Premme 83
programming 35–41, 43, 45–46, 49; food 64–67, 72; and physical appearance 75–76, **79**, 82; producing your own 57

randomized controlled trials 14
Ravings by Rae 83
Refashion Co-Op, The **78**
relative risk 16
Resch, Elyse 59
resources 58–59, **68-69**, **77–80**, **82–83**

Saguy, Abigail 59
Salaime, Samah **77**
Sandoz, Emily 59
Sara Laughed **79**
science of weight loss 13–14
self-presentation 77–84
sewing projects 78
sexual activity 75
Shakesville: Fat Fashion feature 83
Silverstein, Daniel **79**
simple dress **77**
Simply Be 83
Sioux Chef, The **69**
Six Items Challenge **77**
sloppiness 76, **80**
space alien viewpoint for mindfulness 45

strategies for weight loss and body change 3, 7–10, 19, 23, 28; evaluations of 10; science of 13–14; v-shaped outcomes of 13–14
"stress eating" 14–15
swimsuit 45, 75, 79, 82–83, 86–87

tastebuds 29, 31
television 36, 40–43, 57
Torrid 82
traditional dress **77**
travel 75
Tribole, Evelyn 59
triglycerides 26, 28, 32

Uniform Project, The **77**

values 7, 22, 24, 43, 86, 94, 96; and barriers 87–92; case examples 20–21, 23; embodying 74–83; and foodways 67–70, 72; and producing programming 57–58
variation in weight loss 13

Wann, Marilyn 59
We Love Colors 83
weight-based abuse 7, 26, 40, 75, **78**, **80**
weight cycling 25
weight gain: causes of 13–15, 17
weight stigma 17, 25, 28, 46, 59
Well Sewn Style **78**
wheelchair users 44

yoga 58
yo-yo dieting *see* weight cycling

Zero Waste Daniel **79**

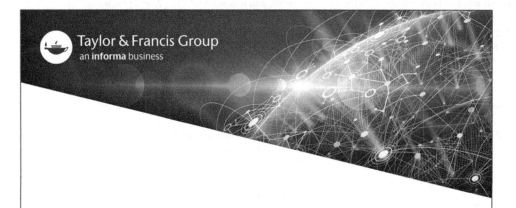